BOUNDARIES

5 Steps to Getting Your Life BACK

DON MINGO

BOUNDARIES

Copyright © 2017
By Don Mingo

Published by Faithway Publishers LLC
Springfield, MO 65807

Faithway Publishers is a publishing house dedicated to publishing books with high family values. We believe the vision for Faithway Publishers is to provide families and individuals with user-friendly materials that will help them in their daily lives and experiences.

It is our hope that this book will help you discover truths for your own life and help you meet the needs of others. May you be richly blessed.

Faithway Publishers
2131 W. Republic Rd. PMB 211
Springfield, MO 65807
417-889-4803
email: lee@faithwaypublishers.com
www.faithwaypublishers.com

Book and Cover Design: Lee Fredrickson

ISBN: 978-1-947828-00-1

Printed in the United States of America

FAITHWAY
PUBLISHERS

CONTENTS

ACKNOWLEDGEMENTS

To the many people in my two pastorates struggling with addictions, thank you for the privilege of opening your lives to me. I've done my best to keep your identities confidential. Your tears and victories find themselves in these pages of *Boundaries – 5 Steps to Getting Your Life Back.*

To my son Donald, for your participation in the formative thoughts of writing this book. Those many conversations over three shot extra hot Venti Toffee Nut Lattes find coffee stains on many pages of this book. Someday, perhaps, we will deal with our coffeeholic addictions. Someday.

To my son Daniel, Media Pastor at Sherwood Baptist Church, your thoughts and information about media, apps, and internet technology find their way into Boundaries. Our many conversations together aiding and guiding me in writing this book encourage a father-son relationship both rich and gratifying.

To my son Dennis, Youth Pastor at Twin Cities Church in Grass Valley, California, your guidance in the challenges our youth face today helped provide urgency for writing and developing this resource. The struggles youth face today seems almost unprecedented. Oh, and thanks for the coffee too! You and your older brother are my caffeine enablers!

To Keith Bassham, thank you for encouraging me to write. Your encouragement that day, sitting in your office, was a cool cup of water during a parched and thirsty time. Resourcing, and editing

Boundaries – 5 Steps to Getting Your Life Back is much more than just appreciated.

To the men who asked me to speak on this subject in a breakaway session during their Men's No Regret Conference more than three years ago. That day, God touched me to write after men listening to my presentation pressed me to put into print that which I put forth in words.

To my sweet, supportive, lovely wife. "Oneness" describes our many years relationship. Our many years together are years of oneness. Kathy, within these pages you will see your essence and presence. If I had to do it all over again, I would do life with you.

To God, my Father, who, through His Precious Son, forgives and heals us from our many afflictions. You enable us to live better lives. May it be so!

INTRODUCTION

*"No man knows how bad he is until he has
tried very hard to be good."*
C. S. Lewis

My breakout session title for the conference was, "Purity in Your Digital World." I felt the title would reduce the attendance. Men don't want to admit their crossing over a boundary into the presence of this dark world. They fear discovery.

To my surprise, with more than 20 other breakout sessions being offered simultaneously, at least 30 men either attended my session or spoke to me afterwards about their addiction struggles. Those who attended the breakout heard my BACKS presentation. BACKS is an acronym for Boundaries, Accountability, Confession, Knowledge, and Sorrow, a spiritual mind renewing process to help people break out of their addictions. BACKS centers itself in a cognitive, spiritual, truth renewal process taught in Romans 12:1-2,

> "I plead with you to give your bodies to God because of all he has done for you. Let them be a living and holy sacrifice—the kind he will find acceptable. This is truly the way to worship him. Don't copy the behavior and customs of this world, but let God transform you into a new person by changing the way you think. Then you will learn to know God's will for you, which is good and pleasing and perfect."[1]

One of the men asked me, "Why don't you write a book about

this BACKS thing? I've never quite heard anyone teach on this quite like you did today. It was very helpful to me. I mean, I'm doing a lot of things to help me deal with my addiction, but something like this might help. I've struggled with an addiction for a long time." During lunch, several other men approached me on the subject. One man said, "If I can't deal with this thing, it's all going to be over—my marriage and life." That comment pierced my heart like an arrow. As I left the conference that day, a voice seemed to say to me, "Don, you are going to write that book!"

This book, *Boundaries – 5 Steps to Getting Your Life Back*, is a result of trying to help Christian men and women for the past thirty years deal with their addictions. *Boundaries* is also my own personal survival growing up in a family riddled by too many addictions to discuss here.

Rarely a week goes by without a desperate person sharing their struggles with addictions. *Boundaries – 5 Steps to Getting Your Life Back*, presents five key transforming steps to changing your attitude, heart, and mind about your addiction. Changing the way you think, helps change the way you act. BACKS is the 5 Step transforming approach offered. BACKS is my safeguard as well. Developed over the years, it helps prevent me from falling and becoming what the Apostle Paul called "a castaway."[1]

Stories of healing, restoration, and fulfilling relationships seem few and far between these days. Those suffering addictions in the church, often experience only partial victory at best. Many are angry, bitter, confused, and unaccepted in churches today. Unable to escape the clutches of their addiction, they become castaways. Probably the most damaging of all realities. Reeling from guilt and failure, they too often give in and give up. Lurid addictions, base practices, and habits take them far beyond anything imagined when they first ventured into the alluring world of addiction. Later, unable to think about anything else, addiction becomes their constant dark companion ruling their lives. What once seemed a generous friend now is a menacing dragon seeking to destroy their very existence.

Through the years, I grieved watching many fine people standing on the decks of their once hopeful and beautiful lives, only to slip into the deep, dark, icy waters of ruin. The damage is catastrophic to spouses, to children, women, men, churches, and communities.

In 35 years of ministry both in South Africa and the United States, in every people group we assisted, addictions in one form or another afflicted all our churches. Pastoring ten years in the United States, and serving as a Fire-Police-EMS Chaplain, witnessed similar tragic consequences.

A young man, buckling to peer pressure, tried Spice. The synthetic marijuana opened the dragon's door leading to Josh's destruction. Witnessing his alarming rapid downward self-destructive spiral was a traumatizing experience for many involved. The pain and misery inflicted upon parents, family, and friends were, well quite honestly, beyond description. Josh will never recover to what he once was.

Personally, raised in an alcoholics' home, both mom and dad, addictions of every kind afflicted and wounded us all. As I look back over the years, trauma filled all our lives from the youngest to the oldest. My sweet wife of thirty-eight years shares a more egregious upbringing.

Whether opioids, alcohol, illegal drugs, porn, gambling, or social media, addiction pushes many into untold misery and destruction. Most addictions, not all, begin with a single decision to cross over a boundary into unknown horizons of intrigue. Of the many encounters with individuals, many reach for additional helps asking for one more life preserver to hold their heads above addictions' cruel waters. *Boundaries – 5 Steps to Getting Your Life Back*, is such a preserver.

Why Addictions are Such a Problem

During many sessions of listening to Christians struggling with various addictions, several common factors emerged. These factors are partly upon which BACKS is based.

First, few boundaries preventing access to their addiction functioned well. If barriers existed at all, they were porous at best. An extremely high percentage of people gained access to whatever addiction was ailing them. A sliver of availability always appeared when temptation's urge presented itself. "I tried." Or, "It wasn't my fault." Or, "I just couldn't resist," often waited on the other side of addiction's availability. Defences constantly proved inadequate. A conditioned mind always provided paths to access.

Next, **Accountability plans and partners were porous too.** Oh, they enlisted accountability partners. Prepared plans to prevent addiction's accesses existed. But, their lifeboat continually took on water due to its lack of integrity. Doctors' instructions were regularly ignored. "What did your doctor say," I asked. "Well, they said to do this or that . . . but, I don't agree with them." Prescribed medications were misused, abused, or not taken. Also, accountability partners proved weak, inconsistent, and, at times, enabling. Often, accountability meant sitting with another equally struggling person, suffering the same malady, both together excusing each other's deficits.

When it came to the Bible, many Christians participated in a haphazard practice of Scripture reading, if they read the Bible at all. Studies show a high percentage of Christians rarely read the Bible.[2]

Amazingly, with Scriptures readily available on varieties of media; Bible illiteracy is extremely high. Sadly, one of the most powerful weapons in a person's arsenal to overcome addiction is ignored. "For the word of God is alive and powerful . . . It exposes our innermost thoughts and desires" (Hebrews 4:12).

Also, **confession, one of the highest attitude-changing disciplines of the Bible, was rarely practiced.** While regrets were plenteous, confession didn't exist. "I'm so sorry . . ." accompanied many tears. Yet, one of two extremes often prevailed. Self-loathing or self-victimization became the mantra. Either, "I hate myself—I'm worthless," or, "It's not my fault—I can't help myself," was the tag many identified themselves.

The art of biblical confession is little understood today by the Church. It's transforming power is rarely attempted. Often seen as merely penitence and punishment, its transformational power is experienced by marginally few. Confessions are usually weak attempts of prayer to an unknown Person. "God, you know I've got this problem. I can't help myself. Help me help me. Amen." Or, conversely, "God, I'm such a crumb. I'd be better off dead." Neither extremes example biblical confession and its renewing purpose. In confession is renewal!

Also, **knowledge and understanding of the far-reaching tentacles of their addiction's consequences remained unexplored**. Many explaining their plight, simply did not understand the costs of their bondage. Little understanding existed of the process taking place in their addiction by their addiction. Clueless to the damage done to countless people around them and themselves, ignorance was not bliss, but rather blistering.

While self-loathing, excusing, guilt, or victimization

abounded, few showed true "godly sorrow" for their decisions, habits, and actions. Godly sorrow is the final key to getting your life back. Godly sorrow is different from guilt. It ensures victory. When one feels the way God feels about their addiction, transforming recovery is within reach.

Getting Your Life Back Depends on Understanding and Applying These Principles

This five-step BACKS approach offered in the following pages emerges from assisting countless people over the years. During 35 years of pastoring in South Africa and the United States, initially, many early attempts to help people were met with little success. Repeated failures occurred regardless of the accountability tools, filtering tools, and accountability groups utilized.

Ten years of serving as a Chaplain in two fire departments and one police department in Minnesota provided perspective and training. My heart often went out to the many suffering from the results of their addictions. I often thought, "What a shame. What might have been if . . ."

Through sorrows, struggles, frustrations, pain, failures, and losses, I offer *Boundaries'* humble approach; BACKS. It's a five-step process that can change your life! It's practical. It's understandable. It's mind changing. It's transformational. It's a spiritual, five-step guide to assist you in gaining control of your life once again. BACKS, while containing Bible principles, is not exclusively Christians. BACKS presents a spiritual, cognitive, soul renewing process to help you in conjunction with your current approaches. *Boundaries – 5 Steps to Getting Your Life Back* is not intended to replace your doctor's, therapist's, or leader's guidance. For the Christian, *Boundaries* adds an additional layer of help, enabling you to defeat your Addiction Dragon.

Through a spiritual truth, mind renewing process, *Boundaries* helps change one's spiritual and cognitive thinking about issues that are driving many towards their addictions in the first place. You must understand that only through the Holy Spirit's help, renewing of your mind, and changing your practices, can freedom be grasped.

How to use this book

Boundaries offers several components of spiritual discovery, recovery, and healing. The components require time and thought. I suggest you start journaling your thoughts, musings, and meditations as you read each chapter. Every chapter concludes with:

- Key Essentials
- Scriptures for Reflection
- Ponderings
- A Prayer to Pray

Key Essentials

It is only through mastery, repetition, and prayer that your mind is renewed to live above addictions clutches. It takes six months of repetition for an action to become a habit. Good habits change how one thinks. Changing how one thinks changes the way the person acts. Changing how a person thinks changes the person. Changing is what it's all about! Master the following pages. Repeat each step every time you struggle. Through continual prayer and transformation of God's Word, victory is yours should you choose to grasp it. "Thank God! He gives us victory over sin and death through our Lord Jesus Christ" (1 Corinthians 15:57 GWT).

Victory is yours should you choose to seize it!

Scriptures for Reflection

Reflect on all the Scriptures at the end of each chapter. Study them. Learn them. Think about them. The Word of God, the Bible, contains power towards changing your mind in a rethinking healthy way. As you change how you think about your addiction, you will gain control, with God's help, over your actions and thoughts.

Ponderings

Spend considerable time on the Ponderings. Write your thoughts down. Write out your answers. I beg you. Please do not skip over them. Talk with yourself. Meditate, think, ponder, and muse. Working through Ponderings helps you battle the war going on in your mind, affecting your thinking and actions. When you are tempted, go to Ponderings. Write. Replace thoughts pushing you towards your addiction to thoughts offering an escape.

A Prayer to Pray

Pray each prayer with your whole heart. Pray the prayers repeatedly. Pray them each time you are tempted. Pray them each time you feel a leaning towards your addiction. Learn to approach God during your times of deepest need. Experience God's love and acceptance. God wants you to win over your addiction too. He's your biggest supporter. Through prayer, you will find God's availability in your times of deepest failures and fear. Learn to lean on Him, experiencing his love and concern for you.

"So let us come boldly to the throne of our gracious God. There we will receive his mercy, and we will find grace to help us when we need it most" (Hebrews 4:16).

If the written prayers don't suit you, write your own prayers. Keep the prayers with you. Use them often. Effective targeted prayer is one of the secrets to victory.

The Heart of the Book

Most of all, master Chapters 6-10 that presents BACKS! Within these chapters are your blueprints for victory. They may provide all you need in the battle against your dragon. The step-by-step approach offered is geared towards changing how you think. With this approach, you can find a new mind and heart. The BACKS way of thinking is where you will find change.

Use Notes and Bible References

There are many websites, resources, and Bible verses in the end notes at the back of the book. Go to the websites. Get knowledge about this issue. Understand it. Read and study all the Bible verses. Many struggling with addictions grasp very little of the Bible. Speaking with recovery groups and small group leaders, I am constantly reminded of biblical illiteracy today in the church. The very book the Church claims to believe, the Bible, is practically unknown to many sitting in the pews on Sunday morning. God's Word possesses the power to transform your life. "For the word of God is alive and powerful. It is sharper than the sharpest two-edged sword, cutting between soul and spirit, between joint and marrow. It exposes our innermost thoughts and desires" (Hebrews 4:12).

Begin a Journal

A psychologist friend of mine often requires his patients struggling with trauma to journal their experiences. He says, "I'm not quite sure what it is about journaling, but writing is therapeutic and healing."

Write, write, write! Writing and journaling will assist you in learning to think differently about all that plagues you.

Most of all, the goal of *Boundaries* is to guide you into submitting all of your being to God under the Lordship of Jesus Christ. It is my prayer that this intensive work will give you hope, the vitality of relationship, and fulfillment. It is only in and through Jesus Christ that we have our life, hope, and breath. May you experience victory in Him. This is my earnest desire and expectation for you! Be blessed.

Key Essentials

BACKS, with God's help, can aid you in getting control of your life again. BACKS may assist an addiction sufferer regardless of the addiction. While a single addiction is dealt with in the later pages of *Boundaries*, apply BACKS to your struggle. BACKS, as an added tool, may help you immensely to finally gain victory over your dragon.

Scripture for Reflection:

"By his divine power, God has given us everything we need for living a godly life. We have received all of this by coming to know him, the one who called us to himself by means of his marvelous glory and excellence" (2 Peter 1:3).[3]

"I want to know Christ and experience the mighty power that raised him from the dead" (Philippians 3:10).

Ponderings

1. What encouraged you to begin reading *Boundaries*?

2. How do you view the idea of a "Boundary?"

3. How has God given you everything you need for a godly life? Do you believe this? How do you believe the above verse true or not true?

4. Describe your relationship with God.

5. If you were completely free from addiction, what might your life look like? How would it be better? How would it be more fulfilling?

6. What changes do you need to make to improve your life in this area?

7. What changes can you make right now, today, this very moment?

8. How does this offer you hope? Or, little hope, Or, perhaps, no hope?

Prayer

Dear God,

You are everything I need for living a godly life. This is what Your Word says.

I struggle to understand this.

Help me know that Your strength and power is greater than any addiction I am experiencing.

Help me experience Your presence. This is a gift that I can receive by coming to know You.

Help me to know You, oh God. Let me see and know Your glory and excellence.

May Your presence shine upon me and dry up the desires that destroy so many things.

Help me to know and experience your Son Jesus Christ—through the same power that raised him from the dead, I can be delivered from my bondage.

And, God, You have given me Your powerful holy Word. Wash and scrub my life through the renewing of Your Word.

So Be It! – Amen"

CHAPTER 1

HERE'S THE THING ABOUT DRAGONS

*"It does not do to leave a live dragon out of your calculations
if you live near him."* —*Gandalf*
J. R. R. Tolkien – The Hobbit

An addiction sort of resembles a dragon. At least to me. Dragons are not real, of course, but let's pretend they are for a few moments, and you will soon get the connection. This chapter is not long, but you don't want to skip it.

A dragon, when first acquired, is like most infant animals: they're cute. My step-dad once acquired a cute puppy that grew into a huge mammoth beast. The half German Shephard-Doberman once ripped his custom van to shreds after only leaving the dog alone in his vehicle for fifteen minutes. The dog did $6,000 worth of damage to his beloved vehicle.

In the beginning, in infancy, most animals appear as great pets. Dragons are like that too. Young dragons are not that much trouble, not that much trouble at all; at first. They are easily kept hidden away and taken out when you want to play with them. They are so small you barely notice. They understand your needs. A newly acquired dragon is there for you. It heeds your every call. Controllability is a major advantage of owning a young dragon. You can take it out and put it away at the most convenient of times.

A young dragon provides many benefits. They're mythical, or so it seems, taking you to fantasies never imagined. A dragon takes you on exciting voyages. Exciting, deep, dark, exotic places await you—places you didn't know existed. Your young dragon offers unconditional acceptance, too, at least in the beginning. And this little fellow will take you just about anywhere you want to go, when you want to go, and whenever you want to go, for as long as you want to stay.

Acceptance is a young dragon's greatest virtue. Your dragon accepts you just the way you are. There are no conditions. There are no responsibilities. You may present yourself any way you like. Whether in a bad mood and a bit grumpy, you're accepted. Are you happy and excited? Perfect! There's no nagging, no fault finding, no conditions. Yes, you can just be you.

There are zero entanglements! None of the problems that plague relationships present themselves in the beginning. No fuss, no mess, no problem—whatever you want. Your only responsibility is to you and your young dragon. Once you gain access to the dragon's world, it's free sailing from there! No arguments—none of that, "my needs, your needs" stuff. No, "my time, your time;" none of that. No! It's a no-hassle relationship! No arguments! No in-laws! No family! No problems! It's up to you. Total control! It appears perfect in every way.

And why not? It's all about you. Your dragon can thrill you with its magical powers beyond your wildest expectations. It's somewhat of a shape-shifter, too, a transformer if you will. Your dragon will be anything YOU want it to be. It appears in any form you conjure up! And, it's so much more! It's sort of like the starship holodeck from Star Trek. Remember those *Next Generations* episodes where the captain and crew could escape the rigors and stress of running the *Enterprise*? Just a few decks away the holodeck offered fantasy-based getaways. A young dragon is such a place—at least in the beginning. You just imagine it, and you're on your own private holodeck.

The cost of such a relationship, in the beginning, is minimal. There isn't a lot of money to lay out. There is no cost commitment. There is no spending on anything or anyone except yourself. But, perhaps best of all, there are zero relational struggles and hassles.

Also, you can treat your dragon in any manner you wish. Speak kindly. Speak harshly. Use the dragon. Abuse the dragon. Accuse the dragon. Neglect the dragon. Not a problem. In the beginning, your dragon is just happy to spend time, any time, with you. You are special.

A small dragon is a perfect companion. It introduces you to other wonderful companions. Your new dragon-friends enjoy your company. These new friends appear the most beautiful compliant people you've ever met. And here's the thing—they find you beautiful in every way. In fact, they love you, want you, and accept you just the way you are. Their only purpose is to serve and love you. Your dragon's mission's statement is:

"To Serve You, To Love You—That is All I Do."

It gives, expecting nothing in return; at least in the beginning. It's almost too good to be true. Yes, a young dragon seems perfect in every way. It's a wonder to behold. Dragons are quite the rage these days. It seems everybody has one, two, or three of them. Then, however, they start to grow. That's when trouble starts. That's when the dragon begins to take control of your life, exacting an ever-increasing price for its services. That's when your DRAGON becomes your ADDICTION, growing into an eight-story building.

Key Essentials

The Dragon is so satisfying, so fulfilling, so promising, and oh, so deadly. Yes, deadly. Like Satan himself, the Great Serpent, he knows every weakness. The Beast understands when best to tempt and lure you away from goodness, happiness, and wholeness. This Leviathan marks out a path of exciting adventure. Yet, the Addiction Dragon, your Dragon, causes much painful, and tearful destruction. Unleashing yourself from the Dragon requires a redirection of worship. Through new worship comes transformation and eventual loss of desire for the Dragon.

Scriptures for Reflection

"I plead with you to give your bodies to God because of all He has done for you. Let them be a living and holy sacrifice – the kind he will find acceptable. This is truly the way to worship Him. Don't copy the behavior and customs of this world, **but let God transform you into a new person by changing the way you think.** Then you will learn to know God's will for you, which is good and pleasing and perfect" (Romans 12:1-2).

Ponderings

1. Remember how you first met your dragon?
2. How long have you been together?
3. What was your relationship like in the beginning?
4. Describe your relationship now.
5. How do you feed your dragon?

6. How does your dragon influence you?

7. Where do you think your dragon wants to take you?

8. What damage is this dragon causing to:

    Your spouse?
    Your marriage?
    Your family?
    Your work?
    Your intimacy?
    Your self-respect?
    Your health?
    Your walk with God?
    Your income?

9. What good thing has God done for you?

10. What do you think of that little word "let" in Romans 12:2?

11. If you were completely transformed as described in Romans 12:1-2, what might you look like?

12. How can you change the way you think about your addiction?

Prayer

"Dear God,

Help me see my dragon for what it truly is; something that I worship. At first, it was exciting, but now it causes me grief. Help me understand how it seeks to control me. Show me how I can give myself completely to you, oh God. Show me how I can worship you.

Help me see all the good things you have done for me. Help me to realize my new life in you.

Teach me to use my body, mind, and soul as a means of your grace and glory.

My dragon is not my master. You, God, are my master. I want You in your grace to lead and guide me. I wish to live under your liberty and freedom. I want you to be my master.

Show me the way.

So Be It – Amen."

CHAPTER 2

MATT AND MATTIE

Sunday morning worship service finished, and with the last handshake, it was time to go home for Sunday lunch, football, and a nap. As I turned the corner on my way to the office, I saw a young couple waiting. I had seen the looks on their faces before. This couple was in trouble. There was a problem. The wife's expression told me it was serious—very serious. I saw fear, pain, and suspicion. In his face, I saw gloom. Then he spoke.

He began, "Pastor, can we talk with you a while?" Heavy eyelids and a famished stomach would have to wait. These types of sessions never ended quickly or cleanly.

We sat. The signals were easy to read. There were signs that I had seen numerous times with many other couples. In her eyes, betrayal and fear peered through her pretty young face. His face was weighed down with shame, and guilt, with a look that said, "I'm busted!" He didn't make eye contact with his wife or me. He just looked straight down at the floor as he mumbled through his words.

After more than 30 minutes of uneasy posturing and trivial chitchat, I knew we were heading nowhere. So, gently I interjected, "Matt, have you crossed a boundary here?" The unexpected strange question produced a unique, bewildering response. It's a coaching question I ask often. "Boundary," always produces a vast array of surprising responses. Matt answered, "Ah, a, WHAT?" I repeated, "Matt, did you, are you, violating some boundary of your commitment to your wife?"

With that, the sniffles started, and tears streamed down his wife's smooth, soft face. "Yes, yes …" as she forced out her words. Through cupped hands over her face, she mumbled, "I found just some of the most awful stuff on his computer, and now I'm scared—scared for myself and my little girl."

Matt crossed two boundaries. Leaving familial's boundary, he traversed pornography's boundary into a torrid world of bondage. Matt crossed over into porn. He stood between two worlds clearly marked by boundaries, relationship, and vice.

Sitting before me was a beautiful, young, 23-year-old woman, already in her second marriage. To her left sat Matt, now silent, looking down at the floor. For Matt, what started out as a casual adventure into the dark side of the Internet years before, while in high school, now posed dangerous threats to their marriage. Looking down into his lap, he muttered, "I really don't know what to do." Matt was in over his head.

Matt (not his real name) was in trouble. Night after night, he busied himself in the darkly lit corner of his study. At first, he controlled his viewing. No one ever knew, but over time viewing consumed him. Now, he could no longer hide it. He feared his insatiable appetite possessed more power than he did. His dragon now became an enemy to slay him rather than a companion to accompany him. He needed help.

The "work," he pretended to be doing into the early hours of the morning, was nothing more than hours of surfing the Internet for one more lurid adventure. One more experience. One more escape.

At first, there was some level of morality. Matt refused to go to certain sites, the hardcore sites, the "really bad sites." But, the bar kept falling from one new low to another. "I, I … really never meant to look at some of that stuff, but now … now, well, I just don't know," he cried out. Matt didn't realize the level he had sunk in his dark viewing habits. Matt was hooked on porn, and it devoured everything he valued.

What concerned Matt's wife Mattie (also not her real name) was the "ickyness"[4] of some of Matt's viewing. She cried, "It's all so "icky."[5] Whenever we make love, I feel so dirty. It's not love at all. It's something else. Something else I don't like. I don't want it anymore. I don't want him anymore."

She continued, "And, now he wants me to do stuff that I don't want to do, and look at stuff that's just, well …"

Matt's head dropped as his eyes looked straight down to the floor again.

Mattie continued, "What really bothers me is that some of the women look so young, like young teenage girls, like little girls maybe just 14 or 15 years old." She paused, seemingly summoning the courage for her next statement, "They look like my daughter! I'm really worried about my daughter!"

Matt immediately objected interrupting, "I would never do that to her!"

Mattie rolled her eyes, looking to the ground as more tears rolled off her face.

Staring straight into Matt's eyes, I gently pressed a probing question, "Matt, how do you know you'll never cross over that boundary? Look at the many boundaries you've crossed over already.

Do you understand where this dragon called "porn" wants to take you?"

Matt responded sheepishly, "Well, I, I, guess I don't know … really."

Then I asked, "Do you know what Jesus said about this?" That caught Matt off guard again. Surprised, he shot back, "Jesus talked about porn?"

"Yes, absolutely," I continued. "Jesus taught that all sexual immorality comes from your heart—and that includes porn."[6] When you cross a boundary into pornography, so many bad things—horrible things begin to happen."

Matt grunted, "Well, I don't know if I agree with that."

I laughed. I couldn't help it, and I playfully answered, "So, you don't agree with Jesus?"

Matt looked down to the floor again.

"Matt, please look at me," I gently encouraged. As he slowly looked up, I asked, "Did you know the Bible teaches that whatever you give your heart to is the person you become? In fact, that is indeed the person you are becoming right now. You, my friend, crossed a boundary into a dark, lurid place. The dangers there are immense. There is no upside. Your porn dragon will ultimately devour everything you value. You are becoming that which you never imagined. Do you see this?"[7]

Matt, now both ashamed and perplexed, replied, "No, not really."

Quietly and gently I said, "Matt, that is why the Bible says to guard your heart. All the stuff of life, both good and bad, flow out of your heart. Never let anything cross your heart's boundaries that cause harm."[8] It literally means, to put a boundary, a wall, a barrier around your heart.

Mattie erupted, "Am I going to have to divorce him, too?"

Her words clearly told how she coped with the problems. In her mind, the solution was just to leave, quit, and begin again. Mattie was afraid. She was covered with fear. This fear is an emotion wives often exhibit when confronting a husband caught in egregious porn. The fear she was no longer desirable. The fear she couldn't compete with porn's allure. The fear of porn's effects on her relationship and family. The fear of what the bedroom felt like. The fear of losing a husband, their marriage, and a friend. Finally, there is the fear of losing intimacy.

As one woman said, "We no longer make love. We just have sex—unfulfilling, mechanical, sex."

Women fear the changes porn produces in their husbands. "That man is not the same person I once knew," is often the cry. As porn's presence deepens, a couple, once in love, become just strangers inhabiting the same house.

Fortunately, hope was desperately crying out, not only for Mattie but Matt, too.

"Mattie," I began, "When you look at Matt he is not sin on two legs. There is goodness in him. There is a good man deep down there desperately trying to get out of this predicament. There is a man who crossed over a forbidden boundary and is now surrounded by darkness, unable to get out. There is a man who wants to love you and your daughter. A man right now who is a bit lost. He just needs some help to find his way; a better way, the best way."

Turning to Matt, I challenged, "Matt, when you bring porn into your marriage, you defile your marriage bed.[9] In other words, you make your bedroom a dirty place. It is now a place where Mattie does not want to be with you."

Mattie was nodding in agreement.

I continued, "It's now probably her least desirable room in the house. Your bedroom! You're frustrated about that, but you are the one to blame because you make your wife feel undesirable, unwanted, and tainted. And, Matt, here's the issue. When you leave the boundaries of marriage and cross over into porn, you unleash a most destructive element into your life. I call it the dragon.

The very thing you want, and that both of you want, is allusive now, because, at least in part, of your porn. This is not love. Are you willing to begin making the changes necessary to correct all of this? You must make decisions to return to loving your wife more than loving yourself and your dragon."

During our sessions together, Mattie shared that her first husband delved into heavy pornography. He began having affairs, and shortly after the birth of their first child, Mattie divorced him. For Mattie, finding a decent guy didn't seem possible. Men were all the same— icky, sex crazed beings who always wanted more sex than any one woman could provide.

However, I assured her that inside of Matt existed a good man who wanted to love her. He was just snared, like so many other men, by his own lust.[10] Totally unaware of the incredible addictive powers of pornography, he became its captive. All addictions seek to enslave their followers. He needed help. They needed help. It was going to take time, lots of time, both theirs and mine.

After more than two hours, I assigned Matt to a life coach to help him begin dealing with his porn habits. As we developed a practical guide for his living a porn-free life, one of my best coaching friends agreed to begin meeting with Matt weekly.

That first week he knocked on Matt's door at 5:00 a.m. on a Friday morning. Matt opened the door in a near coma, totally unprepared for Chuck! Chuck, in the way only Chuck could say, proclaimed, "Well, good morning, my friend! You will be ready for me the next time I come to pick you up. Our sessions will always be on Friday at 5:00 in the morning! You have time to surf porn all night, but now you will make time to begin disciplining yourself to become the man you, your wife, and your children can be proud of! The man you really want to become deep down inside. Go get dressed, and don't make me wait next week."

Chuck began assisting Matt in the art of boundary building. Discipline was Matt's first lesson. Through discipline, Matt learned to say, "No." Discipline is the first step to overcoming any addiction. There is the discipline of seeking help, following a therapist's advice, listening to your doctor, the ability to control one's behavior and accept responsibility for one's actions, and completing that 12 Step Program, etc.

I love Chuck! He is the greatest mentor and life coach of men I've ever known. We need more life coaches like Chuck in the Church!

Waking him from his slumber, Matt and his coach went to a local coffee shop, and the first of many sessions began. Four years down the road, Matt and Mattie's story seems a successful, happy one. Matt is porn-free currently, and hopefully forever. He returned into the safe, fulfilling boundary of marriage. His sexuality is now a gift to his wife to love her and to meet her needs. He no longer consumes it only upon himself.

Mattie is also happy. In return, she loves Matt. They are beginning to experience the fulfillment that only truly loving one another can provide; a true love that is so much more satisfying than anything a dragon offers. Matt began learning the true meaning of "love." True

Bible love is a necessary ingredient for rebuilding broken relationships. Matt began learning about the characteristics of truly satisfying love as outlined in 1 Corinthians 13:

Love is patient and kind.

Love is not jealous or boastful or proud or rude.

Love does not demand its own way.

Love is not irritable.

Love keeps no record of being wronged.

Love does not get happy about injustice.

Love rejoices whenever the truth wins out.

Love never gives up.

Love never loses faith.

Love is always hopeful.

Love always endures through every circumstance.

Key Essentials

Matt and Mattie faced huge challenges in learning how to love. Matt's love was taking place primarily within himself, nourished mainly by his own desires for self-satisfaction. Matt willingly, although perhaps unknowingly, left the safe boundaries of his marriage to Mattie. Mattie's love reached for rescue in the stormy waters of fear. Love does not excel in either of these deficit situations. Only through redirection, recommitment, and reconnecting could their marriage survive. Love embedded in self is doomed to failure. Love rooted in biblical love excels, bringing satisfaction and fulfillment.

Scripture for Reflection

"Such love has no fear, because perfect love expels all fear. If we are afraid, it is for fear of punishment, and this shows that we have not fully experienced his perfect love" (1 John 4:18).

Ponderings

1. Can you identify with Matt and Mattie?

2. What part of their story speaks to you? How does it speak to you?

3. What advice might you have given Matt?

4. What advice might you have given Mattie?

5. What do you think about Chuck, the Life Coach?

6. What do you think of this type of approach to helping men dealing with pornography?

7. What do you think about the statement, "Matt needs to love his wife more than he loves himself and his porn?"

8. What steps do you need to take to better love your spouse, family, and friends more than porn? Write these steps down. How can you begin to act upon your steps?

9. Matt has been porn-free for a number of years. He and Mattie are happy and doing well. What do you think about this?

10. Do you think you can ever come to a place of porn-free living like Matt? Why or why not?

Prayer

Dear God,

You know where I am in this problem. There is nothing hidden from you.

You desire so much more for my life than the scraps this world offers me. I've learned a self-gratifying love from this world. A love that is not real. A love that focuses on me.

Teach me your love; true love.

Please, God, lead me in the path of righteousness for your name's sake.

Show me the way I need to go.

Give me victory in this area of my life.

Help me to come to a place where my life is free from pornography and the damages it does to my life and those close to me.

Help me learn to live and to trust in you. Enable me to love you, my family, and my neighbor.

So Be It! – Amen.

CHAPTER 3

THE PORN DILEMMA

"Like a muddied fountain and a polluted spring is a
righteous man who yields, falls down, and compromises
his integrity before the wicked."
Proverbs 25:26

The host of late night television show made a joke about pornography—it is a common theme among comedians. His punch line was, "And, you know what that is? Well, that's called men!" The crowd erupted into laughter and applause.

I turned to my wife Kathy and said, "Yes, that's right. That's men. They laugh about it, but we see the ruined lives, marriages, and wounding of the innocents because of porn. It's no laughing matter; it's a tragedy." Pornography is a devastating problem on many levels. This crisis muddies families, homes, schools, communities, and societies around the world.

Studies also indicate more than 50 percent of all pastors also struggle with entrapment to pornography.[11] Several years ago, Steve Farrar in his book, *Finishing Strong*, sounded the alarm when he made a troubling discovery. He wrote,

"A number of years ago, a national conference for church youth directors was held at a major hotel in a city in the

Midwest. Youth pastors by the hundreds flooded into that hotel and booked nearly every room. At the conclusion of the conference, the hotel manager told the conference administrator that the number of guests who tuned into the adult movie channel broke the previous record, far and away outdoing any other convention in the history of the hotel."[12]

One missionary agency interviewing prospective missionary candidates reported 80 percent of their male applicants voluntarily indicated a struggle with pornography. The agency said, "We no longer ask if the male applicant has a problem with pornography, we assume it. We ask them what their level of porn viewing is."[13]

Porn is the rampant unspoken addiction of the church. Churches across the first-world landscape are being eaten alive by the dragon. It's perhaps, our largest addiction. With increased access to technology, it's gaining access among developing nations too. Many young adults sit in church today accessing everything and anything on their smartphone. They know more about this subject than any previous generation at such a young age.[14] Even though it's rotting the very fabric of our souls, in most churches, it remains a taboo for discussion. It is time to confess this horrible deficit and to deal with it on a church level, confessing our sins to one another.[15]

There are, of course, many good books on this subject. *Boundaries – 5 Steps to Getting Your Life Back* is, I hope, the first of several uniquely helpful aids offered to lift God's people out of the despair of addiction. As a comprehensive, practical, and spiritual guide, this *Boundaries* edition offers hope to rid one's life of porn. Forever!

Perhaps, no verse in the Bible sums up the reality of porn-living better than Proverbs 25:26. Man after man muddies his life crossing porn's boundary to drink at poisoned, polluted waters of pornography's well. Yes, at first, the waters are cool and refreshing. However, waters from this well create a ferocious thirst that is impossible to quench. The more one drinks, the more insatiable one's desires become. As one drinks its poison, it seeps into the very fabric of the man and changes his personality. As he yields, he falls and compromises his integrity. Porn muddies a person sometimes beyond recognition. Ultimately a person doesn't recognize who he or she has become. Worse yet, a person doesn't understand the process transforming them into the person they despise.

Look at Proverbs 25:26. One part of the verse describes the actions, and the other part describes the result. Let's take actions first:

"A righteous man who falters before the wicked is like a murky spring and a polluted well."

The Man Who Yields

Yielding and giving in is where it starts. The first yielding opens the world of pornography. Traveling down life's road, it becomes easier to yield to porn's constant traffic. Many of those counseled, told that at first, they felt indignity when viewing porn. They instinctively knew it was shameful and wickedly wrong. As they viewed more, their attitude changed. The raunchier became palatable and acceptable. "At first, I watched just once or twice a month. But, now it's like every day," is what I hear from most.

When men begin to yield, they cite a host of self-justifying reasons for their pornography viewing and actions surrounding it. They make excuses for doing what they know deep down inside is unseemly. The Bible teaches us that we are responsible for these actions. James, the half-brother of Jesus, wrote in his epistle:

"And remember, when you are being tempted, do not say, 'God is tempting me.' God is never tempted to do wrong, and he never tempts anyone else. Temptation comes from our own desires, which entice us and drag us away. These desires give birth to sinful actions. And when sin is allowed to grow, it gives birth to death" (James 1:13-15).

Many men experienced the last few words of these verses—sinful actions, growing sin, and eventual death. Losing their marriages, dignity, and worse, they ask, *"Why did God do this to me?"* God gets the blame for that which He is not guilty.

The Word of God points the finger of blame towards us. We willingly yield ourselves to temptation. It is a willful act. What tempts a man originates from his own sinful desires; what he really wants deep down inside. Our addiction offers us a pathway to that which we truly desire deep inside.

Otherwise, it would prove no temptation at all. If it didn't tempt you, you wouldn't be bothered by it. Many men, speaking of porn, often believe themselves more victims than culprits. They offer hosts of self-deluded excuses to remove their culpability for their thoughts and actions. James clearly teaches the opposite is true.

The Man Who Falls Down

The man who yields to porn, no matter how secure he believes himself, is stumbling. Think about a young child just learning to walk. The child repeatedly falls as he or she learns how to walk. Perhaps a better picture is that of an older adult too weak and frail to walk without fear of stumbling and injury. The *New American Standard* uses the phrase "***gives way***." It literally means to totter, shake, or slip. In his "falling down," he lives a life that shakes, totters, slips, and goes down over and over again.

The Man Who Compromises

First yielding, then "falling down," and then a man willingly gives into that which is not good. He releases his integrity reducing himself significantly in the eyes of others. Most of all, he reduces himself in his own eyes. Compromising often involves justification for an action. He thinks, "This is okay. I can control it. It's not so bad. Where is the harm? No one knows."

Even before he is found out, he literally gives away his integrity described as "blamelessness" and "justice." "Integrity" carries here the idea of innocence. This man, having yielded and fallen, is no longer blameless or innocent before the world. He is guilty. Just one of the crowd. There is nothing that sets him apart. He dwells in the gutter. He lacks a moral compass. Often, his guilt matches people he previously disdained.

The Muddied and Polluted

An older word carries the idea of both these terms. He is now "sullied." The Hebrew word for polluted is *shachath*, and it means "decaying" or "rotting."

I remember the day I visited Ladysmith Provincial Hospital while living in Ladysmith, South Africa. I visited an old man stricken with gangrene. His leg was amputated because it literally rotted due to severe complications of diabetes. I'll never forget the smell encountered entering ward 10. The smell of rotting flesh permeated everything. Close to the extremely ill man lay at least ten other people, all suffering from the same malady. The sight and smell overwhelmed me.

It was a heartbreaking scene. I was sympathetic to their suffering, but that experience also taught me something. First, these sufferers didn't notice the smell of their rotting bodies. They were so, ill and sick, they became accustomed to their horrendous odor. Second, in many cases, their tragedies were preventable if treated early. Pornography is much like gangrene in its effect. Its moral decay rots the person from within. It creates such a stench that the afflicted is totally unaware of its presence. Then the sufferer falls, slain by a preventable spiritual disease.

It Plays Out Before Others

Here's the sad part. A man's compromise of his integrity eventually becomes visible to many around him. The NASB translates part of this passage, "Like a trampled spring ..." The picture here is one of a pure fresh artesian spring flowing out into the open. Its waters once pure, cool, and pleasant to taste are now cloudy and muddied from hordes of boots trampling through it.

King David's life, the second king of ancient Israel, mirrored this passage almost perfectly. Despite all the great accomplishments of David's rule, one severe criticism was written on his epitaph at his death. It concerned his actions with Uriah the Hittite. David murdered Uriah to cover up his affair with Uriah's wife. Many terrible consequences followed because of David's hideous sexual escapades. Perhaps the worst consequence can be found in the words, "He gave the enemies of God cause to blaspheme ..." (2 Samuel 12:2). Some translations translate this phrase, "He showed such contempt for the Lord..." Regardless of his great works, David is remembered for sullying himself and his character. His actions turned some of his best friends against him.

Looking at the prominence of pornography, particularly among men in North American churches, the website Crosswalk.com claims that more than half the men in churches sully themselves regularly in porn.[16] Covenant Eyes©, an Internet accountability, and filtering company, gives figures that are staggering.[17] Facts, figures, and statistics show the severe problem of pornography in our churches. It has set up camp in the pews! And, it is not just a young man's problem.

In his "Open Letter to the Church," noted Christian leader and author Charles Swindoll sounds a warning,

> "Our churches are in significant trouble. I'm not talking about financial trouble or having too few staff doing too many things. Comparatively, those are easy problems to solve. This trouble concerns a severe disease that is eating away at our congregations, perhaps even some of our own leadership, from the inside out. Men and women, from adolescents to senior citizens, from all walks of life, have succumbed or are at risk, and more are becoming infected every single day. The problem is pornography, especially Internet pornography. Without your knowing, it could be eating your church alive. And the scariest thing is ... you may not realize the extensive damage it's causing."[18]

During my last pastorate, we started a class for men struggling with porn. We sort of hid the word "pornography" by using the term "purity." We called it a Men's Purity Class. It was a dangerous gamble as no man wants his personal struggles in this area revealed. Our men's committee decided to conduct that class on Sunday morning. Although I did not think the timing was the best, amazingly enough, 30 men showed up ranging from 17 years of age to a gentleman who was 84 years old! In fact, ten of the men attending were over 50 years old! One old gentleman over 70 years of age caught me off guard, after a class, with these words, "Pastor, I view porn on my TV all the time." Another honest 30-something man asked a rather interesting question during that first session. He inquisitively inquired, *"So, what's so wrong with porn? If you're careful to control it, and use it wisely, I mean what's so wrong with it? It does seem to possess a lot of benefits."*

What's So Wrong with Porn?

Here are just a few facts about Internet porn you should find startling:

1. 50% of men and 30% of women regularly view porn.[19,20]

2. 97% of self-identified Christian men have admitted to seeing porn.[21]

3. 80% of Christian men have no filtering system installed on their computers or smartphones.[22]

4. 55% of married Christian men view porn at least once a month.[23]

5. 25% of born-again men erase their browser history to conceal porn.[24]

6. 50% of pastors are involved in porn.[25,26]

7. Nearly two-thirds of men admit to accessing pornography while at work.[27]

8. 88% of scenes in porn films contain acts of physical aggression.[28,29]

9. 49% of the scenes contain verbal aggression.[30]

10. 56% of divorce cases involved one party having an obsessive obsession with Internet porn websites.[31]

11. 66% of porn performers have sexually transmitted diseases.[32]

12. Porn decreases sexual satisfaction, enjoyment, and performance.[33]

13. Porn lowers one's view of women.

14. Porn desensitizes the viewer to cruelty, turning men into predators.[34]

15. The average American will see 15,000 sexual references a year on television alone.[35]

16. Porn often is a world of manipulation and control.

17. Porn views people as mere objects of sexuality rather than people with value.

18. Internet porn normalizes wild sexual fantasies, encouraging sex offenders.[36]

19. Porn has a neutering effect on men, leaving some men sexually impotent.[37]

20. Pornography and depression are often linked.[38],[39],[40]

21. Regular viewing of pornography is a leading cause in men's erectile dysfunction.[41],[42]

22. Regular viewing of pornography over a long period of time has gradual devastating effects on the viewer.[43]

23. Studies show a link between declining marriages and pornography viewing.[44]

24. Pornography over stimulates the brain.[45]

25. Excessive pornography viewing produces withdrawal-like symptoms when trying to abstain from viewing.[46]

26. Pornography is not real sex.[47]

27. Couple those observations with some research from the people at www.fightthenewdrug.org who talk about the effects of porn:

28. Porn is addictive—it controls you.

29. Porn actually changes your brain by creating new neuro-pathways in the brain.[48]

30. Porn definitely affects behavior, and negatively so.[49]

31. Porn does not increase one's sex life; it actually ruins it.

32. Porn kills love, hurts your partner, and leaves many men lonely.

33. Porn is not fantasy, but rather a world flooded with drugs, disease, slavery, trafficking, rape, and abuse.

34. Porn often leads to sexual assault against women and children.

35. Behind the cameras of the porn industry is a violent, brutal world of subjugation.

36. Pornography damages and destroys families.[50]

Psychiatrist Miriam Grossman in her article, "A Psychiatrist's Letter to Young People" noting the once popular book and movie *Fifty Shades of Grey*," sounds the alarm. She states, "There's nothing gray about Fifty Shades of Grey. It's all black. I help people who are broken inside. I ask questions, and listen carefully to the answers. One thing I've learned is that young people are utterly confused about love—finding it and keeping it …. In the real world, this story would end badly."[51]

Kathryn Casey expresses concern about men like Christian Grey, the main character portrayed in this book: "What I find unsettling is that in Christian Grey I see the attributes of so many of the men I've written about over the years, the ones who abuse and sometimes even end up murdering their intimate partners. Experts have said for decades that rape is more about control than sex. What I've seen over and over again is that a man who needs to dominate, humiliate, and physically abuse a woman isn't a hero. He's not doing it out of love. That guy isn't the man of any woman's dreams. He's a mistake, one she won't end up rehabilitating but fleeing."[52]

Once, when I mentioned the book, a church member of an Evangelical Bible-believing church took me to task on this issue. I was challenged, "You're taking this *Fifty Shades* thing way to serious! If you'd just read the book …"

I interrupted, "Ah, I did read portions of the book, and I can tell you that any man caught doing to Ana what Christian did could end up in prison for sexual assault. Would you want your daughter dating a man like Christian?"

The conversation abruptly ended.

Now is offered *Fifty Shades Darker*. Porn is always darker and deeper as one sinks into its abyss. It never satisfies pushing one to cross another boundary empowering the dragon towards more power and destruction. As one dives deeper, seeking a satisfying experience, darkness delivers pain and emptiness. The shades of porn produce darker, empty, unsatisfying lusts. And, porn is a leading cause of the ever-increasing group of young male porn viewers unable to obtain an erection. Addiction.com holds that excessive porn viewing reduces young men's libido, encouraging a reliance upon Viagra and Cialis.[53]

Recently, a conversation with a Christian man in his mid-30s reinforced the tragedy of porn's influence in his life. At the end of his second marriage, he said, "I've been heavily involved in porn for years. I got started in it while in the military when I was stationed in Iraq. I can't make love. I can't get aroused with my wife anymore. Nothing seems to do it for me. I know it's ruined my life, and now my second wife has filed for divorce. I never dreamed I'd be divorced twice. I'd love to give it up, but I can't."

So, here the ultimate tragedy of porn unfolds. Porn is about sex. Sex is about intimacy. A man wants to *see* erotica. A woman wants to *experience* erotica. And, in the end, both experience neither.

Pornography destroys any prospects of true intimate relationship. There is no sharing. There is no closeness. There is no fulfillment. There is no love. There are just faceless digital imagines supporting a "world wide web" of suffering and exploitation. Porn is about taking, not giving. In the end, there's just a miserable, angry, guilt-ridden, dirty-feeling guy alone with himself, his smartphone, and his computer.

Now, this addition of *Boundaries* is not to convince you of the dangers of pornography with facts or statistics. There is a wealth of good material out there with such information. *Boundaries* is not trying to guilt you. It's not trying to scare you into life changes. That never lasts very long anyway. *Boundaries* is not preachy, launching a thousand Bible missiles your way. Such tactics, solely on their own, initially appear successful, but rarely last more than a few months. Neither is the aim of this book to judge you or condemn you. The purpose of *Boundaries* is to help you see the perils of your porn, overcome it, forsake it, live above it, and enjoy a truly intimate, satisfying sexual relationship as God intended!

Chances are if you're reading these words you already sense the damaging nature of porn, either in your life or that of another. Perhaps, you are in the throes of battle with your own dragon. The dragon is strengthening at an exponential rate. Subduing it seems daunting, if not impossible. You've failed many times. Maybe this scares you. It should.

You are rightly concerned about what's constantly in your mind, thoughts, and emotions. You struggle to associate with the opposite sex on any level. Everything is filtered through your pornographic lenses. Your work is affected because you sexualize those around you.

Sexualization occurs to such a degree that it snuffs out any possibility to relate with people other than in a sexual manner.

Meeting another soulmate and forming a long lasting, mutually nurturing relationship is impossible. You are pornographized (I sort of just made up that word, but it works). Every appealing person is viewed through your sexualized lens.

Through constant Internet viewing, you've rewired certain parts of your brain to think the way it does. You're trying to kick your habit, but you're failing. Even with the help of some great programs, accountability groups, and good books, your dragon is winning.

You meet your dragon often. Most engagements begin with initial euphoria. Then you suffer another defeat, retreat, regret, and repeat. Here, hopefully, you will receive help. In these pages, you will find your answer to this devouring problem. Here, right here, you can take a deep breath and begin breathing hope. Take heart. This book is for you. There is a way. Victory waits for those willing to learn, train, and apply. As the Apostle John said, "Greater is He (God) that is in you than he that is in the world" (1 John 4:4 KJV).

The Reason Porn is Such a Problem

During many sessions of helping mostly men struggling with porn, several common factors reinforced BACKS.

Again, few barriers preventing porn access existed in most of their lives. If barriers existed at all, Internet filtering, for instance, they were porous at best. An extremely high percentage of men, especially pastors, had no internet filters installed on their smartphones, computers, and other electronic devices. Most guys trusted themselves solely in their battle against pornography.

Accountability plans and partners were again porous too. Oh, they enlisted accountability partners. They prepared plans to prevent porn access. Yet, their moral compass continually lost its way, lacking a true North to guide them. Weekly, they found themselves at a coffee shop or in group sessions wringing their hearts out to accountability partners after yet another defeat to their dragons.

When it came to the Bible, most men didn't read at all, let along memorize Scripture. Again, studies show that a high percentage of Christians rarely read the Bible.[54] Today, the bestselling most accessible book of all time, the Bible, is little read nor accessed by men struggling with porn, or any other addiction for that matter. And, men, as a general rule, don't like to read.

And, while some were in some sort of program to deal with their porn, it clearly wasn't working. They continued to dabble with pornographic Ouija boards. Christian men repeatedly crossed the boundaries of purity and integrity to drink from porn's trough of bloody, putrid waters despite their best efforts to abstain.

When it came to the confession of sin, most men generalized their confessions. Sadly, they excused themselves repeatedly for "falling to porn." There was always some rationalization as to why their porn problem was really, "not that bad" or "unavoidable." Many men struggled to discuss the issue with their wives, hiding their bondage until caught.

A very old professor, during my early years at Bible college, warned young prospective pastors of the dangers of dabbling at pornography's well. Two things he repeated.

"Gentlemen, when you entertain the serpent of *porneia*, and *pornos* (Greek words Jesus used for fornication and sexual uncleanness) mark it down; you will get bit. And, when you get bit you will get sick.

And, eventually, everyone around you will know your true condition. They will probably know what you've become before you do. You will lose everything because *porneia* will slay you right where you stand."

His second point always followed the first. "And gentlemen, when it comes to sexual sin, Christian men initially turn from sexual sin, get on their hands and knees, and crawl away hoping they'll get caught. And, usually, they do." Unfortunately, over the years, this truth played out in many of the young men in that class. Years down the road, those once young freshmen disqualified themselves from ministry due to sexual deviancy beyond anything they had imagined possible.

Boundaries seeks not only to deliver you from porn, but encourages you to submit your sexuality within the boundaries of the Lordship of Jesus Christ. This is the high goal. In doing so, you will discover the prize—becoming a true disciple of Jesus Christ (Luke 9:23).

Key Essential

See the destructive powers of pornography—your end. It sullies and destroys so very, very much. Stripping you of your integrity, it tears down everything you truly desire. Ruining your relationships, it robs you of joy. BACKS looks carefully at your weaknesses and lack of boundaries in your approach. Only by taking a hard look at yourself, and soberly knowing where to begin, can you deal with your problem.

Scripture for Reflection

"And he said to them all, If any man will come after me, let him deny *(boundary himself)* himself, and take up his cross daily, and follow me" (Luke 9:23 KJV italicized text mine).

"But you belong to God, my dear children. You have already won a victory over those people, because the Spirit who lives in you is greater than the spirit who lives in the world" (1 John 4:4).

Ponderings

1. What are your thoughts about the word "sully?

2. How is pornography sullying your life and relationships?

3. What do you think about some of the statistics and figures given related to pornography?

4. How do they surprise you? Startle you? Scare you? Concern you?

5. Where do you fall into these statistics?

6. How is pornography far more reaching and consequential than just personal viewing of it?

7. What's your confession of pornography? Describe it.

8. How is your personal approach to dealing with pornography successful?

9. How is this same approach failing?

10. How much power does your Porn Dragon possess over you now? How does it control you?

11. What Bible verses do you memorize? How often do you quote Bible verses to yourself when tempted to look at pornography?

12. What might a porn-free life for you look like today?

13. What might your life look like a week from now porn-free?

14. What might your life look like a month from now porn-free?

15. How about a year from now?

16. What changes are you going to make?

Prayer

Dear God,

Help me take pornography seriously.

Help me see its devastating effects.

Help me see the immense damage it's causing; to myself, to those around me, and to those enslaved by it.

Help me see the ruined lives left in its wake.

Change my heart, oh God. Help me see anew. Mold and make me into the man you desire me to become.

Help me develop a plan to combat and defeat this evilness.

Give me the hope for the victory you have promised – the victory only you can give.

So Be It! – Amen.

CHAPTER 4

ADDICTION OR BONDAGE?

"Our valour is to chase what flies; our cage
We make a quire, as doth the prison'd bird,
And sing our bondage freely."

William Shakespeare (Cymbeline III,iii, 42-44)

Let's talk about two terms quickly. Do we call a porn habit, addiction, or bondage? Addiction carries multiple layers of definition. Addiction is often used to describe a chemical dependence. It can also refer to repetitive, negative, damaging behaviors. The word is widely used to describe just about any destructive repetitive behavior. Skilled mental health professionals seek to help people on this level. Yet, in the medical community, there is great debate as to whether or not sexual addiction is actually an addiction or learned behavior.[55] While the term addiction is acceptable and legitimate within some contexts, a Bible term better suits our purposes.

The word *bondage* is perhaps more accurate than addiction, at least from a Bible perspective. The Apostle Paul warned, "Stand fast therefore in the liberty by which Christ has made us free, and do not be entangled again with a yoke of *bondage*" (Galatians 5:1 NKJV). In the New Testament, bondage translates the Greek word *douleia*,

53

the condition of a slave,[56] and cognates of the word often have to do with slavery in the New Testament. Strangely, there are actually two diametrically opposed concepts in that word, and little middle ground between them.[57]

Powerless Slave?

In the ancient world where Paul lived, slavery formed the very economic fabric of society. Slavery was a brutal, forced form of submission of one person to another. Slavery often occurred through the military conquest of one people over another. For the slave, it effectively ended liberties, freedom, and happiness.

There were several ways people became slaves in the ancient world. The word bondage is used 19 times in the New American Standard Bible to describe the life of a slave in the Old Testament. The Hebrew word *abodah*, translated bondage, usually referred to captives. *Abodah* describes Israel's 400 years of captivity in Egypt.

Some individuals in the ancient world willingly gave up their freedom, to become slaves, and that is reflected in the etymology of *abodah*.[58] Bondage or slavery implied one who willingly gave up their rights to another. Giving up rights to become the property of another occurred for a variety of reasons. Often it made economic sense to willingly become the property of a kind, generous, wealthy slave master who, in return, provided for the slave's needs. It also carries the idea of giving up one's rights for the rights of another, or to accommodate oneself to a particular occasion.[59]

Most of the time *abodah* people were born, purchased, or captured into slavery. As property, they possessed virtually no rights. They lived and died knowing nothing else. As parent-slaves, the birth of their children was nothing more than the acquisition of property from parents to slave owner. Bondage was unbending, unyielding, and often unbearable. Slavery's bondage formed an inescapable part of the ancient world.

It is in this light that Paul seems to use the term bondage or slavery as it is often translated in many versions of the New Testament. Bondage, in Galatians 5:1, refers to a power far beyond one's ability to escape, and in that case, Paul is describing what it meant to be under the power of a false belief system, as opposed to liberty found in Jesus Christ. Romans 8:21 uses the term differently. Paul there describes the situation of all creation, under the bondage of decay and sin, anticipating a release or redemption when the New Heaven and New Earth appears in the end times.

The Bondage of Pornography

Pornography is bondage. It is difficult to break loose from its power. It possesses its own version of decay and sin. It exploits. It desensitizes. For some, their slavery began as they were lured into it innocently during their adolescent and teens years. Others were captured during viewing and experimenting with porn later. Some walked into porn with their eyes wide open. The results are all the same, as one young man shared, "It's like I am chained to this thing, and can't seem to break loose."

Kevin Johnson of *USA TODAY* interviewed an incarcerated 52-year-old retired Navy communications specialist serving a 20-year term for possession of child pornography. Published Friday, February 11th, 2015, the article reports of a Navy communications specialist, John, who had transformed his desktop computer, laptop, electronic notebook and multiple external hard drives into vast reservoirs of illicit images featuring sexually compromised children, some as young as one-year-old. [60]

The Navy vet said, "I regret all of it."[61] Police reported that the man possessed terabytes upon terabytes of child pornography. One officer said it was more than anything they had ever seen or known. John reportedly spent years acquiring the materials. He described his pursuit of child porn as an obsession no less real than the heroin addict's search for another fix.

"I couldn't stop," he said. [62] And, he remembers almost exactly when he "crossed over to the dark side."

"It piqued my curiosity more than anything," he said.

The investigating officer reported, "John 'indicated that the stuff bothers him.'"[63] Asked if he'd ever do it again, he smiled, replying in the affirmative. John's tragic, disturbing end is a story of personal bondage and slavery. John is a slave to his Porn Dragon. It continues to slay him.

Slave-Doulos or Doulos-Servant?

The New Testament offers a new way to view slavery. Paul likes to use *doulos*. You can easily see how this word resembles the Hebrew word for bondage. It can describe the type of slave bondage depicted above. Paul, however, likes to use the word to describe his relationship with God.

Paul viewed himself within the boundary of a happy *Doulos-Servant*, not a slave. In that context, the word describes a person completely and unconditionally surrendered to another. Though often misunderstood by many who are thinking of slaves suffering harshly, Paul's use of the word indicates richness in relationship and high personal value. It describes oneness with God through Jesus Christ. *Doulos-Servant* is used with the highest dignity of an individual in the New Testament—namely, of believers who willingly live under Christ's authority as His devoted followers.[64] *Doulos* is God's boundary-answer to our slavery, ourselves and our sin.

Slaves or Servants—No Middle Ground

The use of the word *doulos* in the New Testament always finds its usage in the term "slave." Few other words are used in English translations. Yet, in the Greek language, Paul's use of the word clearly indicates a double meaning. There are only two options in Greek—servant or slave. There's no middle concept.[65]

There are only two options than, for a Christian believer. You are either a slave to sin[66] or a *doulos-servant* of Jesus Christ. Rather than being forced into bondage, a *doulos-servant* enjoys actual friendship with Jesus Christ.[67] This same word, by its application, implies a clear choice. You are either a forced slave to sin or a servant-friend of Jesus Christ. Being Jesus' servant-friend comes with many wonderful, amazing benefits.

The New Testament richly describes the depth of that relationship with Christ with several metaphors and similes:

1. New Creations – 2 Corinthians 5:17

2. Chosen – 1 Peter 2:9

3. Masterpiece – Ephesians 2:10

4. Justified – Romans 5:1

5. Beyond Condemnation – Romans 8:1

6. Children of God – John 1:12

7. A Temple – 1 Corinthians 6:19

8. Connected, as a Vine and Branches – John 15:5

9. Friend – John 15:15

10. Members – 1 Corinthians:27

11. Citizens – Philippians 3:20

12. Children of Light – 1 Thessalonians 5:5

13. High Position – Ephesians 2:6

14. A Good Work – Philippians 1:6

15. Sweet Smell – 2 Corinthians 2:15

16. Receivers – John 15:16

17. Spiritual House – 1 Peter 2:5

18. Chosen Ones – Colossians 3:12

19. Sealed – Ephesians 1:13

20. Seal of Ownership – 2 Corinthians 1:22

Personal choices of living within boundaries or crossing over forbidden boundaries, into dangerous territory, determines your bondage or freedom. Entering a *doulos* relationship with God provides boundaries, releasing you from bondage to pornography forever. Men often express how dirty, damaged, guilty, and disappointing they are to family, friends, and God. One man shared, "I am so unworthy." That's bondage. Staying within safe *doulos* boundaries ensures fulfillment.

Do you want freedom and release? It's in Jesus Christ that renewal, rebirth, and victory are accessible. In friendship boundaries with Christ, a believer is satisfied, freed, and empowered.

Key Essential

Living under the influence of porn is bondage. It means serving porn as a slave to your sinful desires. Seeing your special place in Jesus Christ brings deliverance. Knowing who you are in Christ removes the guilt that pornography produces. Understanding your special relationship in Christ cultivates a *Doulos-Servant* relationship. This is who you are—a very special person created to serve God in His Son Jesus Christ. This is where God intends you to live, in the palace of a privileged relationship, and not in the gutter of the world's troughs.

A choice awaits you. Will you choose to dwell within the safe boundaries of a *doulos* relationship with Christ, self, family, and spouse?

Scripture for Reflection

"But you are not like that, for you are a chosen people. You are royal priests, a holy nation, God's very own possession. As a result, you can show others the goodness of God, for he called you out of the darkness into his wonderful light" (1 Peter 2:9).

Ponderings

1. What are your thoughts about "bondage" and "addiction?"

2. Boundaries – thoughts?

3. What does *doulos* mean to you?

4. Do you agree with the statement that there is no middle ground between bondage to sin and being a servant of Jesus Christ?

5. When you think about your porn, how does it make you feel?

6. When you think about Jesus, does he give you hope/no hope?

7. How does the thought of being released from pornography's bondage give you hope?

8. Are you ready to become a doulos-servant of Jesus Christ?

9. What are the necessary steps you need to take to become a doulos-servant?

Prayer

Dear God,

Help me see the bondage my porn life brings not only to me but all those around me. Help me understand, oh God, what this life of slavery brings. Not only to me, but to my spouse, my family, friends, church, and community.

Show me freedom in your Son Jesus Christ. This is the wonderful relationship you offer me. Help me seize this opportunity.

Take away the damaged guilty feelings of my heart. Those feelings telling me I am helpless, worthless, and alone.

Help me see your goodness, your forgiveness, and, my next steps in you.

So Be It – Amen.

CHAPTER 5

SETTING UP TRAINING CAMP

"God has called us to resist temptation. He has
called us to holiness. He has called us to battle."[68]
"Lay your back into it!"

The Pirate Primer: Mastering the Language of
Swashbucklers and Rogues by George Choundas[69]

"I discipline my body like an athlete, training it
to do what it should. Otherwise, I fear that after
preaching to others I myself might be disqualified."
1 Corinthians 9:27 (AMP)

Ask any successful athlete about the immense suffering they put their bodies through to compete successfully. I've known several people in South Africa who ran the Comrades Marathon.[70] This marathon, run every year at the end of May, is the oldest ultramarathon in the world. The course is more than 56 miles. Almost unbelievable, isn't it?

Competitors pound out thousands of miles running to prepare for this one marathon. They deny themselves sweets, fatty foods, and alcohol. They train through injuries and sickness. They sacrifice recreational time with family and friends. They train, train, and then train some more! Then the day of the race comes. Waking up early, 11,000 people stand ready at the starting line. The pistol fires and they are off and running.

Eleven grueling hours are allotted to complete this race. World-class runners finish in under six hours. And what do they receive for all their troubles as they cross the finish line? A small, rather worthless, medal is all they carry home after their race. That, and a lot of stiffness, soreness, and pain! I knew several runners, after finishing the Comrades Marathon, their toenails turned black and fell off! Yet, every person I've talked with among those who finished the race maintained it was well worth it! Just to finish was more than enough reward!

That approach to training—to finish—is the idea you need to understand in 1 Corinthians 9:27. I "discipline my body," he writes, using the Greek word, *hypoppiazo*, which literally means to beat yourself black and blue. Paul perhaps meant this quite literally. It was a word used in the day for a boxer or athlete handling his body roughly to prepare for competition in athletic events.

The word "disciple" is in the same word family. To be a "disciple" can mean putting yourself through terrible annoyance to accomplish a task. That is, you discipline yourself and make yourself terribly uncomfortable, training your body to perform something most people cannot. Other translators claim Paul was saying he subdued his body, bringing it to slavery. His body obeyed him, rather than he obeying his body. He possessed complete control over his body so that it did not shame or embarrass him and others. Paul feared failure in this area.

"Fear," you say?

Yes. Fear. In the American culture, fear is considered a negative emotion to be avoided. Fear is a bad thing. Yet, Paul, the great Apostle, feared becoming an unfit man to those he was trying to help. He feared failing people closest to him. To Paul, embracing that fear was of great benefit. Fear can become an ally rather than a foe. As one young husband said, "I fear if I continue down this path, I will become that which I do not want to become to myself, my relationships, my marriage, and my family."

Among the Zulu people of South Africa, you can pick up some picturesque African proverbs. Many African proverbs emphasize learning and the acquirement of skill. One says, *"By trying often, a monkey learns to jump a tree."* This proverb teaches that learning is a process of repetition over time.

When faced with a rather daunting task, an older African man might ask a young man, *"How do you eat an elephant?"*

The obvious answer is, "One bite at a time."

The moral lesson offered there is, "When attempting to overcome large obstacles, often a step by step approach is required."

And the way we get there is through discipline: conditioning your body through buffeting it in training. BACKS helps accomplish this.

Barriers, **A**ccountability, **C**onfession, **K**nowledge, and **S**orrow.

BACKS practices renewal of your mind, heart, and soul patterned after a passage in Romans 12:1-2 in the New Testament.

"I beseech you therefore, brethren, by the mercies of God, that you present your bodies a living sacrifice, holy, acceptable to God, which is your reasonable service. And do not be conformed to this world, but be transformed by the renewing of your mind, that you may prove what is that good and acceptable and perfect will of God."

BACKS is the retraining of your mind. It's a complete guide to equipping yourself to meet temptation, your dragon, and defeating it; renewing yourself within disciplined boundaries of preparation and preparedness. It's going to take commitment and work on your part.

As in a soldier's gear, every piece of armament and equipment serves a specific purpose. Every piece requires practice and mastery to ensure protection and success. Can you imagine a soldier entering battle without a helmet? Or, picture a Marine in full combat gear standing on his bare feet. Likewise, many good, sincere men confront their dragons only partially geared, poorly equipped, and unskilled to use that which they do possess.

During my first American pastorate, I served as a chaplain in the local fire department. It was a large, paid, on-call department with over 100 firefighters and five fire stations. In order to help me connect with the firefighters, the chief suggested I go through all the training required to become a certified firefighter.

At first, I was a bit apprehensive. Firefighting was completely foreign to me. Terms like turnout gear, psi, NIMS, nozzles, two-stage pumps, one-stage pumps, reducers, and a host of other words were not a part of my vocabulary. I wasn't in great physical shape either. Just putting on all the fire gear was slow, uncomfortable, heavy, and cumbersome.

Training meant getting into shape to carry almost 100 pounds of gear. We trained and trained and trained. Believe it or not, I learned the technique of donning[71] my fire gear in less than two minutes. When we struggled out on the fire scene as a team, we reviewed the situation that same week, made adjustments, and trained again!

What was needed on the fire scene became routine. You just do your job. The firefighter just did it. Training ensured this.

Lack of training and equipping is why so many men fail in their battle with porn. Regardless of recovery groups, materials, and approaches, much of the gear they adorn for battle fails to bring success. Failure is common because people who are seeking deliverance from porn lack determination, expertise, and skill. Most of all, they lack training.

Repetitive drilling changes how one thinks and acts. Repeating the same act constantly until it becomes habitual is the key to success. Isn't repetition the reason you struggle so fiercely with pornography now? Repeated hours of viewing porn conditioned your brain to think the way it does today. Your will opens your brain allowing images to flood into your heart, images shipwrecking your life. Repetitive pornography viewing is why your brain thinks the way it does today. In reversing this, spiritual repetition is a key factor to overcoming your porn habits.

No amount of weaponry brings success apart from discipline and training. Isn't it interesting how men struggling with pornography have mastered the Internet and all its tools to access porn? Their training to access porn is thorough, ongoing, and dedicated. On the other hand, very little training occurs when battling porn. With the best of intentions and bravery, they continually find themselves outgunned, outmatched, and unprepared for battle. They fail over and over again.

While on the mission field, I lived just a few hours from the 19th century Zulu-British War battlefields in Zululand, South Africa for more than 20 years. There, I learned how brave Zulu warriors fought the British. Under orders of Queen Victoria, British soldiers sought to subjugate all Zulus to her rule. As the British advanced upon Zulu homelands in Natal, the Zulus were forced to defend themselves against the invaders. Armed only with spears and leather shields, they charged in formation into the British lines incessantly. Finally, during the Battle of Ulundi, the Zulus suffered a crippling defeat. As Ulundi, the capital of the Zulu Empire, burned to the ground, soldiers captured Chief Cetshwayo, taking him prisoner and shipping him off to England.

The Zulu Empire never recovered. The Zulus simply were unprepared to battle the British. They did not lack tactics, courage, or strength—they simply could not match arms with their enemies for such a battle. Will, intention, bravery, and spears were no match for cannons, bullets, and the dragoon's charging cavalries.

Most Christian men enter their battles similarly ill-prepared, ill-trained, and ill-aware. Armed with good will, momentary enthusiasm, an accountability friend, and a few Bible verses, they stand in the name of God in front of their dragon only to be slain once again. Scripture talks about the importance of total preparation: "Therefore, put on every piece of God's armor so you will be able to resist the enemy in the time of evil. Then, after the battle, you will still be standing firm." (Ephesians 6:13).

"Standing firm" is a defensive term for a conscious well-thought-out decision to stand. It is a plan of attack with a sense of utmost urgency.[72] The verse points towards an individual decision for a plan of action. It implies a strong wall of defense able to withstand any onslaught against it. It is a military mindset of defending and protecting one's self from Satan.

BACKS seeks to fully arm you to slay your Porn Dragon, or to meet any other addiction for that matter. It seeks to equip you in such a way that you will stand your ground, not giving an inch to the enemy when it strikes! And, as I have already emphasized, it is an approach that requires training. Practicing all of it is the only sure way to secure your borders from enemy hordes trying to invade your heart.

If you're struggling with porn, you need to understand; you are in a battle. This is the fight of your life. It's a battle for your soul, life, marriage, and family. If you lose, you lose. That's it. While victory is easily defined, it is difficult for many to realize. You must forsake your porn viewing, entirely and completely—100 percent porn-free living in Jesus Christ.

Simple prayers alone for deliverance usually don't work. Just going to your accountability group probably isn't enough either. Telling a friend, while good, most likely falls short. Adding content filters to your computer or smartphone isn't enough either. In all of this perhaps you wonder, "What am I going to do? How am I going to overcome this stuff?" Perhaps you're in the self-delusional stage of, "It's really not that big of a problem. I can handle it."

As you learn the BACKS approach, it will require continual practice. Life Coaching teaches me it usually takes six months of continual repetition before a practice becomes a habit. A habit then becomes a way of life. If you look back at the beginning stages of your pornography viewing, isn't that exactly what you did? Through repetition, your pornographic viewing became a habit, and then it intertwined itself within the very fabric of your soul. Now, porn is part of you. It's like an alien attached to your body, sucking your life force from you. The only way to detach pornography's tentacles from your life is to create new neural pathways in your brain.[73] This is part of the renewal process mentioned in Romans 12:1-2.

In a recent article in the *New Yorker* titled "How to Rewire Your Brain for Success," Geoffrey James cites research that explains how repetition can rewire one's brain.[74] His conclusions come from some new neuro-research on traumatic memories by Daniela Schiller. Daniela directs the Laboratory of Affective Neuroscience at the Mount Sinai School of Medicine in Israel. Her research on overcoming traumatic memories causing PTSD and a host of other anxieties is quite interesting. In her research, she found that neuroscience seems to be able to help us rewrite bad experiences remembered in our brains.[75] In other words, by remembering good thoughts and memories, we may be able to rewrite how the brain thinks about bad events and memories.

This is what the Bible talks about in Romans 12:2. "And do not be conformed to this world, but be transformed by the renewing of your mind, so that you may prove what the will of God is, that which is good and acceptable and perfect." That's what we're after. A total renewing of one's mind to discover what is good, acceptable, and perfect. Through the renewing process, unsavory memories can be written over and forgotten.

One man, successful in overcoming pornography, shared, "As I spent more time in Scripture, more time in prayer, more time on good things and less time in pornography, vivid memories of porn began to fade. After a year of being porn-free, I barely experience pornographic imagery in my mind any longer."

This is where you will receive help if you really want it. This is where you allow God to enter your equation. God becomes your focus. God gives you victory in this area. For God is your present Help in time of trouble,[76] your Refuge,[77] your Strong Tower,[78] your Rock,[79] and your Fortress.[80] It is only in God, and through Him that we live, move, and exist.[81] Most importantly, my friend, God is faithful even when we are not.[82] You can count on God.[83] Go to Him often, no matter how badly you feel about your current situation. It is only through Him you will find deliverance. David, the second king of Israel, went to God often in his many troubles. Note his words when in deep distress:

> "But I keep praying to you, LORD, hoping this time you will show me favor. In your unfailing love, O God, answer my prayer with your sure salvation. Rescue me from the mud; don't let me sink any deeper! Save me from those who hate me, and pull me from these deep waters. Don't let the floods overwhelm me, or the deep waters swallow me, or the pit of death devour me. Answer my prayers, O LORD, for your unfailing love is wonderful" (Psalm 69:13-16).

God is your help. Learn to look to Him often. Learn to live in Him. Learn to trust God with all your heart. Learn to stop trying to figure it all out yourself. In every thought and decision you make, look to God. Put Him first, He will direct you in the way you need to go in life.[84]

Key Essential

You must decide to enter training camp. It's your decision. All the coaching and training in the world cannot help until that decision is made. Will you make that decision to commit yourself? Only through subduing and disciplining your body, soul, and spirit can victory be yours. A total renewing of your mind is the goal. It's promised to you. It's available to you.

Scripture for Reflection

"But [like a boxer] I buffet my body [handle it roughly, discipline it by hardships] and subdue it, for fear that after proclaiming to others the Gospel and things pertaining to it, I myself should become unfit [not stand the test, be unapproved and rejected as a counterfeit]" (1 Corinthians 9:27 AMP).

"Be strong in the Lord and in his mighty power. Put on all of God's armor so that you will be able to stand firm against all strategies of the devil. For we are not fighting against flesh-and-blood enemies, but against evil rulers and authorities of the unseen world, against mighty powers in this dark world, and against evil spirits in the heavenly places" (Ephesians 6:10-12).

Ponderings

1. What stands out to you in this chapter?
2. Describe your tactics for dealing with pornography.
3. Where are you failing in your battle against pornography?
4. Are you willing to set up training camp? When?
5. How can you "subdue" your body?
6. What do you think of this whole idea of training?
7. What do you think of the concept for repeating an action until it becomes a habit?
8. How can this change the way you think about pornography? About everything?
9. Are you willing to go through rigorous training?
10. How is God your High Tower in combating pornography?
11. How is God your Refuge? How can you hide inside of Him?
12. How can God become your Strength?

Prayer

"Oh God, repeatedly, I've given myself to this pornography. Continually I fail and fall.

What once seemed my friend is now an evil enemy seeking to destroy me, destroy my family, destroy my future, and destroy my soul.

God, I need your help. I need your strength. I need you.

I need to be made over again. I need to be renewed. Apart from you I will continue to fail over and over again.

Without you, I am defeated.

Without you I am nothing. I am losing this fight.

So, I look to you, oh God, to you and you only.

Be my High Tower, oh God.

Be my Refuge and my Strength.

Save me, God, by your tender love and mercies. I look only to you for strength and deliverance.

Please help me give myself to you always.

So be it – Amen.

CHAPTER 6

BOUNDARIES

"Either we finish them, or they'll finish us! It's the
only way we'll be rid of them!
If we find the nest and destroy it, the dragons will
leave."
How to Train Your Dragon

"Let there be no sexual immorality, impurity, or
greed among you. Such sins have no place
among God's people."
Ephesians 5:3

The first step to battle your Porn Dragon is to look to your protective boundaries. Building impenetrable barriers is essential. This, quite frankly, most men are not willing to do. They go to great lengths to put elaborate barriers in place, marking their boundaries, and yet they repeatedly leave the back door ajar. Deep down, their heart burns for porn. Many men leave an open conduit to return to porn's allure. Proverbs 26:11 illustrates the problem: "As a dog returns to its vomit, so a fool repeats his foolishness."

Accessibility is the Problem

The Great Wall of China is one of the great marvels of the

ancient world. Built over 15 centuries, through numerous dynasties, it spanned over 4,000 miles. The first boundary was constructed by Shi Huang, the first emperor of China who lived between 259 and 210 BC. In the early stages, it served as a barrier to protect one clan from another. Over the centuries, as China's dominance grew, better, stronger, and higher walls were constructed to protect China from her enemies, particularly in the North. As massively impressive as the walls were, enemies breached the walls repeatedly. Armies either went around them, flanking the furthest extents of the walls, or they penetrated the weakest sections. Often, they entered through the portals of the wall, that is, the gates themselves.

In AD 1644, the Manchus broke through the Great Wall and overran China. They did this by bribing a Chinese general of the Ming dynasty to open the gates.[85] The impressively fortified structure built to keep enemies from gaining access failed. The wall, built over many centuries and requiring the labor of more than 1,000,000 people, it turned out, could not withstand the enemy from within. The greatest enemy was not outside the wall. That enemy lived within them.

How Solid Are Your Walls … Really?

My subject, addressing some men at a conference, was *Purity in Your Digital World*. Afterward, a man in his late thirties approached. For better than an hour he maintained that no matter how he set in place personal boundaries for himself, nothing worked. Constantly, he succumbed to his Porn Dragon, never mind, he said, "… how high I built my walls."

After listening to a long list of his excuses, those he learned through repetitive conditional reasoning, I saw his problem. Yes, boundaries were put in place. Yet, his traitorous heart betrayed him. Opening his heart-gate continually, he empowered the Dragon to ransack his heart-kingdom. The height of his personal walls did not matter. His dragon freely slipped through the gaping holes in his defenses. His personal digital world did not have an honest and committed gatekeeper. He wasn't true to himself. He opened his heart's gate continuously to his enemies allowing them to conquer him.

Porous Boundaries

During my time in South Africa, I was always conscious of security. Because of the extremely violent and rampant nature of South African criminality, the country excels in home security solutions. Every night, before turning out the lights, my security routine began. Outside yard gates were locked, guard dogs were released into the yard, security gates were secured, and the infrared security alarm was armed. In each room, there were two infrared detectors. Bedrooms were bypassed to allow us movement at night without setting off the alarm. Setting off the alarm brought an instant armed response from a security company. Whenever we left the house, the system was armed, doors were locked, gates were locked, and dogs were secured. We were safe—or so we thought.

One day, the five of us left the house to go into town. After setting the alarm, I realized the keys to the van were still inside the house. On that key ring were the house keys, too. I pondered my situation, but my young sons assured me there was nothing to worry about.

"We can get into the house dad."

To my dismay, I watched as one of my young sons squeezed through a security lattice on the window. Moving slowly and methodically, low and against the wall, he reached the security pad, punch in the security code, and disarmed the system.

"We've done this before, Dad!"

With the retrieved keys in hand and the system rearmed, we drove into town, straight to the security company, to upgrade our home security system.

Many men struggling with porn employ similarly flawed preventatives. It's just too easy to pry the security bar off the window, crawl on the floor, and reach the security system. Often, they tell about their Internet filtering programs. They employ some smartphone porn preventatives too. They've acquired accountability partners. Some go to recovery groups. The reading materials and workbooks they've purchased fill their backpacks. Yet, at some point, the Internet filter is turned off or bypassed. They find a way to access porn seemingly undetected. They bemoan their plight. They share it with an accountability friend. They promise not to repeat it. Yet, there they find themselves standing behind weak walls, opening their gates, waiting to be slain once again.

Plugging the Holes

Jesus, teaching on such things said, "If your right eye serves as a trap to ensnare you or is an occasion for you to stumble and sin, pluck it out and throw it away. It is better that you lose one of your members than that your whole body be cast into hell" (Matthew 5:29 AMP).

These are very strong words! The teaching here is absolute, complete, and concrete. This is the key to building strong, fortified, impenetrable walls in your body, soul, and spirit. Radical cancer requires radical action! Anything causing you to compromise your integrity must be rooted out and removed—permanently.

Very few church leaders over the centuries taught this verse as a literal amputation, and it seems clear that Jesus' teaching here is metaphorical. If that is so, then Jesus is saying, "Remove the thing that so easily causes you to stumble. Tear it out. Completely uproot it. Get rid of it in its entirety once and for all. It's better to give that thing up now than suffer the eternal consequences that comes with it." Radical action is commanded.

It may mean ditching that smartphone for a dumbphone. Only texting and phone calls allowed! "How can I live without my smartphone?" is the cry. What is your smartphone doing to you now? How is that smartphone sullying your life? Wouldn't removing your smartphone help turn the tide of porn's effects in your life? Perhaps, it means surrendering your computer until good sound habits and disciplines assure personal integrity.

One individual asked his wife to put passwords on their TV provider. He simply could not watch anything on TV that was questionable unless his wife unlocked that program with her password. Too radical you think? What's the ultimate alternative? Think about the end of your present course? I am currently involved in a conversation with a 35-year-old man as I write this chapter. All he's left with is his smartphone and computer. They are his companions. He's lost his wife and family to pornography. He lives in a cheap hotel destitute of relationship.

A friend of mine was diagnosed with cancer several years ago. Her treatment consisted of radical surgery, chemotherapy, and radiation. Not a pleasant experience at all. Yet, after undergoing the radical procedures, she now lives five years on the other side of cancer. Her cancer is currently in remission. She enjoys life, family, and relationships. Think of the results if she had refused to make the decision undergoing her painful treatments. Most of the men I talk with about their porn simply refuse to take steps necessary to "power down" the dragon in their lives. Jesus' words are clear. Remove utterly and completely that thing so easily causing you to stumble and fall. Are you willing to do this?

Removing the Rubble

Probably no city in the world has suffered more attacks than the city of Jerusalem in Israel. It is likely the most fought over piece of ground in the entire world. Hundreds of bloody conflicts took place over this piece of ground, hallowed by so many. Over the past 4000 years, countless numbers of battles were fought in its locale.

In AD 70, under General Titus, the Romans inflicted heavy damage on the walls. Today, the walls visibly tell the story of the repeated destructions. Layer upon layer indicates a tearing down and rebuilding of the walls. Today, the walls existing in Jesus' day, for the most part, are beneath the pavements of the Holy City. When each wall was rebuilt over the centuries, the rubble was first removed. Stronger fortifications were then erected in its place.

If just one breach of your personal walls allow access to porn, what good are your walls at all? They are, at best, perhaps, an elaborate effort in self-deception. What is the thing or things causing you to stumble? Are you willing to remove the rubble in your personal world, repairing any and all breaches in your defenses? What do you need to pluck out of your media life to preserve purity? Where do you need to build, tear down, or rebuilt? Where are the holes in your defenses?

Internet Access: For many porn strugglers, access to the World Wide Web is too easy. Temptation's victory is just one click away. Plugging this hole is essential. Closing open avenues of Internet viewing is imperative. If necessary, eliminate your Internet accessibility completely, at least for the short term. Self-deceptive excuses will argue this is not possible. One man, several years in bondage to pornography, cried, "How can I live without the Internet?" My response, "How are you living with it now?" After a lengthy conversation that ended with him answering his own question, he began a six-month Internet fast. No Internet for six months!

I know successful businessmen who only use the Internet in their offices. They understand that their Internet habits are closely monitored at work. They know surfing porn at work means possible termination. This provides very strong incentives. With this restriction, they severely narrow their Internet access. It is better to suffer the inconvenience than to lose so much more later.

Social Media: Social Media outlets vary in their filtering policies. While Facebook does not allow pornography, there's plenty to muddy one's heart on Facebook if you're looking. A recent search using the keyword "breast" proved this to be true. Facebook can be a friend or foe. Porn purveyors also lurk on Facebook seeking to draw men with suggestive posts and advertising.

While Twitter prohibits the distribution of pornographic material through its medium, it does give a wide berth to the sexual content people tweet. Porn is available on Twitter by users who post pornography. For many struggling with porn, Twitter is just too much temptation. Pictures and images, freely available just a click away, provide too much allurement.

One young Christian man objected, citing all his thousands of Twitter followers. He feared losing his "followers," never again to regain them, if he ceased his tweeting activity.

I probed, "Hal, how many of your followers contact you in any way shape or form?"

Hal replied, "Ah, well, what do you mean?"

"Hal, of your thousands of Twitter followers, how many actually follow anything you do? Or, even care for that matter?"

Many men simply need to close their Twitter accounts. While very careful with my Twittering, I nevertheless was subjected to seeing a picture of a popular female personality's naked body on one of my friends' Twitter feeds. That friend was immediately blocked and eliminated from my followers' list. If you are unable to stand up to such temptations on social media platforms, it's better to abandon them completely. It is better to leave Instagram and Twitter than lose your marriage, relationships, and integrity. Right?

Possible Online Sexual Meeting Sites. The July 2015 hack and release of personal information of more than 33,000,000 people on the social media site Ashley Madison, alarmed many. Ashley Madison is a website for those seeking an extramarital affair. The applicant reveals personal, lurid, sexual information in hopes of connecting with someone equally sexually debased. Thousands of Ashley Madison subscribers feared the consequences of their actions being revealed. "You mean someone might find out about my sordid sexual thought life?" It cannot be overemphasized that anything you put into cyberspace is by definition never completely private. If you're messing around with these types of websites, be prepared for a reckoning day when all is revealed.

Instagram is another wonderful social medium. My family and some very close friends share photos back and forth with this tool. How else could I keep up with my 14 grandchildren—yes, 14! However, just this morning while writing, someone I did not know "liked" a picture of one of my granddaughters. The unknown person was a woman, and her Instagram pictures showed selfies of herself in sexually suggestive poses. She was immediately BLOCKED (meaning that person cannot see nor communicate with me). Now, my Instagram settings are private. Only those following me can see my pictures. If a new person wants to follow me, I must first grant permission. You must be proactive to guard yourself. It is claimed that Instagram is also the number one media of child predators.

Snapchat is currently popular. This messaging application allows a user to post media, but it is visible for only a few seconds.

Question: "What is your need for Snapchat?" What do you wish to share that needs to be hidden almost immediately? Here's a point to ponder. Nothing is truly hidden on the World Wide Web! Nothing! A particular Mega Church forbids any staff member to use Snapchat. "Your choice, Snapchat or your job."

While I was working for the Eagan Fire Department, an officer in the police department explained to me her job in computer forensics. Here's what I learned. There's not a hard drive existing that information can't be extracted from regardless of how many times the drive is wiped. What goes on the hard drive stays on the hard drive, unless the hard drive is completely destroyed.

That's a good thing to remember, and it holds true in all of life. Scripture says, "The eyes of the Lord are in every place beholding the evil and the good" (Proverbs 15:3 KJV). Clean up, close up, and eliminate any social media sites that lure you into wanting to see pornography! Forsake that which so easily allows the allurement of pornography to slay you once again. It's your choice.

Advertisements. Once, while I was scrolling through my Facebook feed, a picture came up on the right-hand side. A label said, "Summer Mission Trips." The picture below the headline was a beautiful and sexually suggestive young woman. Clearly, it was misleading. Adding AdBlocker [86] or other add-on applications to your Internet browser helps with unwanted suggestive advertisements on the sidebar. AdBlocker works with most Internet browsers and social media platforms. Some browsers offer more protection than others. I have found the Mozilla browser to be a good option.

Smartphones. Many men testify to the temptation of sexual imagery on their smartphones. Smartphones are a huge problem. Porn is just a few taps away on your phone! You can carry pocket porn everywhere now if you want.

What to do? The solution is simple.

Exchange your smartphone for a dumbphone if need be. The same businessmen I mentioned before do not own smartphones. In fact, they own flip phones. A few companies are reintroducing the flip phone again. Other companies are toying with the idea. A fashionable, efficient flip phone may be your first and most effective defense.

Some will say, "Hey, that's not very efficient and fashionable."

Here's another way to think about it, "Efficient and fashionable at what?" A thorough examination of all the apps and contacts on your phone can help restrict access to temptation. It may appear radical, but for some, it is not an option. You can live your life without a smartphone.

Apps. For smartphone bearers, eliminating apps on your phone, which allow easy access to questionable images, is a good idea. After having spoken with many men about filtering products for smartphones on the market, one complaint keeps coming up. Right now a comprehensive, effective product to filter porn on a smartphone doesn't appear to exist. The best Smartphone apps out there for smartphone protection and blocking from porn are at www. covenanteyes.com and by x3Watch @ www.xxxchurch.com. These products help, but neither is foolproof by themselves.

Messaging. A pastor friend of mine raved about the people he met on the Internet in chat rooms and messaging applications. He began texting a woman he met on one of these sites. After exchanging texts with her for several months, he "fell in love." One day he left his wife, connecting with his new love. That new relationship lasted little more than a year, and when his money was gone, she left. My friend, with five academic degrees and years of experience in the pastorate, will never return to that vocation.

Too much caution can't be overemphasized here. If I send a text message to a woman on my phone, there is a specific reason for it. And my wife knows about every text message I send to a woman. Thirty years of marriage attests to the success of this approach. I have a businessman friend who is divorced, and his accountability partner reads every text message he sends or receives. His accountability friend pulls his texting records from his phone company. This ensures honesty.

Dating Sites. If you sign up for a dating site while married, you simply ask for the destruction that follows. A man shared, "Well, I was only having fun. It was so exciting and exhilarating to see women online who were interested in me." Care to venture where he ended up? For singles looking for companionship, dating sites offer excellent assistance in meeting people with similar interests. Be cautious when choosing a dating site. The Psychological Science in the Public Interest Journal has an interesting article entitled, *Online Dating – A Critical Analysis From the Perspective of Psychological Science.*[87] It's worth a read as it points out the dangers and ineffectiveness of many online dating sites.

Once, while walking down the hall at church, a young teen blurted out to herself while looking at her smartphone, "Go fish." My reply was, "Plenty of Fish, huh?" Plenty of Fish (technically, Plentyoffish, or POF) is another one of those dating sites out there promising to match someone to an individual's exact needs and specifications. She looked at me, surprised that an old guy knew what was going on in the Plenty of Fish world. I laughed and replied, "Careful you don't catch an ugly carp or devouring shark."

Tinder is another dating app "helping one find a friend." It is very popular with young people. It's a way to meet people in the area. When a profile shows up on your Tinder screen, you swipe right to like or swipe left not to like. If you like the person and the person likes you back, BINGO! There is a match. The problem with these sites is that people are prone to lie and exaggerate about who they are, and what they want. Also, predators troll for contacts on these sites. There are plenty of pimps trying to locate unsuspecting young women.[88]

Emails. Now call this prudish if you want, but any email I send or receive is accessible to my wife. We agreed to do this after witnessing so many moral failures, wrecked marriages, and relationships when Internet technologies began to surface in the 90s. There simply are no secrets between the two of us. You say, "I can't do that?" Very good; what is your alternative plan of action? How will you assure wholesomeness in your email correspondence? Are you thinking this through?

Television Viewing. One of my friends suggested I watch the HBO series *Game of Thrones.* "You'll love the series!" After reading the reviews, guess what the topic of conversation was the next week we met?

I mentioned, "You know that Game of Thrones we talked about last week?"

He nodded, "Yes, what did you think?"

I answered, "Well, Larry, it is filled with nudity, pornographic imagery, sexual situations, sexual acts, lewdness, and graphic violence. If you're watching *Game of Thrones,* you're watching porn." He defensively responded, "Well, yeah, it's maybe, soft porn . . ." I interrupted, "Larry, it's porn period."

Was it any wonder my friend struggled and lost so many battles against his Porn Dragon?

I ask men, "If you enter the coliseum's arena facing lions unarmed, what is your outcome? Will you survive?" That is similar to a Bible question: "Can a man scoop a flame into his lap and not have his clothes catch on fire" (Proverbs 6:27)?

Larry answered in that conversation, "Well, I guess, no, you can't play around with this and not get burned." Exactly right. Yet, Larry returned to porn, and his dragon eventually slew him. Larry's marriage ended two years later. He became a porn predator.

Frankly, even commercials contain soft porn these days. Much of televisions is not watchable. We have grown so accustomed to what we see on the flat screen; all seems normal.

Traveling. Research the hotels you are booking when traveling. There are many porn-free hotels now. Porn isn't as profitable now since it is so available in other formats. A little preparation and research go a long way here. Business travel presents many temptations for sexual encounters. Many business people tell of stories of long trips, lonely nights, and the acquaintances they spent the night with. These were trips that ended a marriage.

A friend of mine travels a lot. He is confronted with sexual opportunities regularly, especially during his business trips to China. To combat this, he makes a call to his accountability partner every day while traveling. His accountability partner asks him three questions:

1. Have you been faithful to God today?
2. Have you been faithful to your wife?
3. Have you been faithful to your purity today?

Wait! You're Going Way Too Far Here!

Some may think this approach puritanical and say, "You're taking this thing way to far." Really?

What if you physically went to a coffee shop to meet a woman you never met before? And what if, on your first meeting, you immediately opened a sexual dialogue. Not long into the conversation, salacious graphic photographs are produced. Let's say you spend your entire time together in sexually explicit company. Okay? And yet, every time you engage your porn world, this is exactly what occurs.

Shoring Up Your Walls

Ironically, the Internet that can get you into trouble can also offer some help as you move out of the porn world.

www.xxxchurch.com – is a site offering many valuable resources. It's an in-your-face Christian approach to dealing with the ravages of Internet pornography. This site offers many forms of help, encouragements, and tools. Some men testify it's the only resource they need. One word of caution, though. They are totally serious in dealing with your slavery to porn. You must adopt a serious, committed attitude as well. Triple X Church might be the most valuable resource in your arsenal outside the Bible! One of their great ministries is coaching men out of porn. Coaching is perhaps the most effective tool used in combating porn viewing. Their goal is for you to live a porn-free life.

www.covenanteyes.com – is more of a filtering resource for protecting one's self and family from inappropriate viewing. It's a great tool to consider. Their smartphone filtering is superior. Many young men I coach testify to me personally about the effectiveness of CovenantEyes for smartphones. Go to their website. Purchase a full subscription, software, and apps for all your devices. It may save your family, marriage, and life. Do it. Put your back into it now!

Some tools you already possess. Always set your browser's search engine to safe mode. It is easy to do. Consult your browser's Help screens for steps. Next, password-protect the safe mode setting so that you can't turn it off temporarily and access porn on your browser. That means someone else will set your safe mode password so that you can't change your browser from safe mode to open mode.

It's ultimately up to you. It is impossible to filter out all porn from appearing on your screen. Even an innocent shopping site or a news site can contain suggestive material. You must become your own filter in those cases. With apologies to William Shakespeare, think about these words:

To view or not to view—that is the question:
Whether 'tis nobler in mind to suffer
The slings and arrows of a fashionless media existence
Or to take up open medias' sea of endless troubles,
And by freely embracing them. To die—to sleep—
No more; to incur thousands of sleepless nights
The heartache, and the thousand unnatural shocks
That my flesh is now heir to. Tis a consummation
Devoutly to be realized. To die,—to sleep,—no more.

Key Essential

It's not a real boundary if you can cross over it. Your defensive walls are useless if the enemy easily penetrates it. Barriers are nothing if you can easily disable them. Look to your defenses. Shore up your walls. Be honest with yourself. Ask someone else to assist you in studying your defenses. You need honest perspectives.

Clear your rubble. Plug the holes in your walls. Build boundaries so securely that not even you can penetrate them. Establish your boundaries to such a degree, so in your weakest moments disabling them is simply too arduous a task. Most of all, shore up your heart's wall with God's mercy, forgiveness, and love. In God's love, you'll find acceptance. In his mercy, you'll discover strength. In forgiveness, true liberty, as you are renewed day by day.

Scripture for Reflection

"Guard your heart above all else, for it determines the course of your life" (Proverbs 4:23).

"But among you there must not be even a hint of sexual immorality, or of any kind of impurity, or of greed, because these are improper for God's holy people" (Ephesians 5:3 NIV).

Ponderings

1. What are hints of sexual immorality that are evident in your life? List them. Go ahead. Be brave. List every inclination of sexual immorality in your heart. Do it. Sobering?

2. Where are your defenses strong?

3. Where are your defenses weak?

4. Identify the breaches in your approaches.

5. What rubble needs to be cleared away to strengthen your defenses?

6. Where might you start to begin clearing rubble today, right now?

7. What continually opens your heart to pornography?

8. What practical changes must you begin to make in your Internet and media viewing?

9. What social media activity must you eliminate?

10. What changes must you make regarding your smartphone, computer, and other digital devices?

11. What conversations must you change or eliminate?

12. What must you pluck out of your life to save your life? Remember Jesus' words?

13. What needs to be cut off to prevent empowering your Porn Dragon? Note: Remember this is not about a literal body part.

14. Who are you talking with about these changes you need to make?

15. Who is going to ensure you make necessary changes?

Prayer to Pray

God,

I must begin to take my pornography habit seriously.

Help me to see the damaging nature of pornography.

Help me see what it's doing to my life.

Help me understand the negative effects that oppress my family.

Show the path to true relationships outside my pornographic thinking.

Show me protections I can use to close open media access to pornography.

Show me where I need to change. Give me the strength to make those changes.

Give me the tenacity to stick with those changes.

Give me someone who will hold me to my changes.

There are so, so many temptations. Help me remove the rubble and close the holes as well as I can.

So Be It – Amen.

CHAPTER 7

ACCOUNTABILITY

"Accountability breeds response-ability."
Stephen Covey

"Dear brothers and sisters, if another believer is
overcome by some sin, you who are godly should
gently and humbly help that person back onto the
right path. And be careful not to fall into the same
temptation yourself. Share each other's burdens, and
in this way obey the law of Christ."
James 5:1-2

I knew the woman who approached me at church. We had spoken
before about struggles she and her husband experienced with
pornography.

"I just don't know what to do!" she began. "My husband goes to
Celebrate Recovery[89] every week, but he still goes back to his porn!"

I carry a high regard for Celebrate Recovery. It's a wonderful
ministry saving thousands of people from addictions. Yet, a crucial
flaw existed in this particular group.

In her husband's accountability group, the leader of the group also stated he continually struggled with pornography viewing. His accountability partner, a friend, suffered the same struggle. Their "accountability" meetings often deteriorated into sessions filled with them bemoaning their mutual plight.

I don't intend to criticize these individuals or their attempts to deal with the porn issues. The facts are clear, a person with the same deficit as another will struggle to offer adequate accountability. That is the problem James 5:1-2 addresses.

Look at the key elements of this verse:

1. ***"If another believer is overcome by sin"*** – Literally, the idea is of one caught or snared in a trespass, someone who is unexpectedly taken from behind. King David describes this exact picture when facing his own sin. He writes, "For troubles without number surround me; my sins have overtaken me, and I cannot see. They are more than the hairs of my head, and my heart fails within me." (Psalm 40:12). It's the picture of someone running away from something or someone. No matter how long or how fast he runs, the faster enemy runner eventually catches up, overtakes, captures, and slays.

2. ***"You who are godly or spiritual"*** – "Spiritual" is a general word referring to the spiritual part of a person. It implies a person living at a level above a weaker person struggling with the same issue. Here is a key element to success in assisting someone who is overcome with pornography. A good accountability partner exhibits mature attitudes and behaviors regarding the weaknesses another person struggles with.

3. ***"Restore"*** – Spiritual people restore others. They do not criticize

and tear down. Restoration is always the goal. To "restore" here carries the idea of setting a broken bone, mending a net, outfitting, or rehabilitating. Restoration aids someone in becoming whole and effective. Again, restoration requires a spiritually mature person to ensure recovery of a weaker person. Two men equally struggling in pornography rarely offer long-term solutions to pornographic bondage.

As a first responder and firefighter in Grand Rapids, Minnesota, my team and I were called to a car accident involving two vehicles and multiple victims. Some of their injuries were serious. Approaching the scene, I saw a severely injured woman desperately trying to help another severely injured person. While her effort was admirable and heroic, she was ineffective. She only worsened the situation, and endangered lives, because she was too injured to help. Only when firefighters arrived on the scene did the injured begin their recovery.

Many accountability partners and groups struggle to provide adequate accountability. Living in captivity to their own porn, the pattern of excusing and pardoning each other for their "failures" and "weaknesses" merges. Again, I am not condemning accountability structures and arrangements, but we must have some straight talk on the weakness of many accountability approaches.

I knew one man who was struggling with porn, and he told me his accountability group leader confessed that he, too, regularly struggled with viewing pornography. I asked him, "Is that group helping you?"

His tragic reply was, "No, it's like two drunks sitting at the bar looking into their drinks whining about how tough life is." Obviously, we need straight talk about accountability.

Spouses as Accountability Partners

Should a wife be her husband's accountability partner? Some categorically state the answer is "No!" In a ministry workshop with 30 other pastors, I mentioned that my wife was my primary accountability partner. One pastor shot back, "Well, my wife was mine too, but I had no problem lying to her about my pornography."

Looking straight at him, I replied, "Well, if we can lie to our wives, gentlemen, the one's we've promised to love and cherish and always be faithful to, then perhaps we can lie to anyone."

When the Internet was in its early days, I signed up for an online service provider. With Kathy, my wife, looking over my shoulder, I started browsing, though it was tediously slow in those days! My first words were, "Wow! This could really get a guy in trouble. Sweetie, I don't want to go there."

Since that day, we've upheld a 20-plus-year agreement:

1. At any time, she is free to examine any of my devices (computer, smartphone, etc.) and all my email and Internet usage. And, she is very good at computer forensics! I can't hide anything if I wanted to!

2. She is free at any time to look at me and ask, "How are your eyes?"

3. Any email or correspondence with a woman is subject to her examination.

4. Anytime I am struggling with "my needs" I can talk with her about it.

5. Anything in my life that concerns her, she is free to bring to me and discuss. This is nonnegotiable. I promised never to get defensive or angry about this.

6. Thirty-eight years of marriage proves the success of this approach for us.

Not all men can enlist their wives as their accountability partners. For many women, their attitude towards their husbands' porn viewing is prohibitive to this approach. One huge problem in helping women deal with their husband's pornography is their feelings of betrayal. Wives' wounds are often deep when learning of a husband's pornography captivation. It's as if she just learned her husband is involved in an affair.

In the spiritual and emotional realm, there is some validity for the wife's sense of betrayal. I've witnessed Christian women divorce their husbands upon learning of it. One Christian woman exclaimed, "Oh, if I caught my husband in that, I'd divorce him. No questions asked." In the light of such action and reaction, is it any wonder Christian men often choose to hide their private lives?

While you may disagree on this point, I think, if possible, it's best for a wife to help her husband deal with pornography. Look at your marriage vows. Don't they communicate some level of accountability?

Pastors as Accountability Partners

Pastors as accountability partners are usually a bad idea. Most pastors simply do not possess enough margin of time for such a task. I learned this when trying to help a young man named Josh. I still feel very badly about Josh to this day. We began together, but he simply needed more time than I had to offer. With more than 500 other people in my congregation at the time, his needs were beyond my abilities to manage. When I stepped back, he felt betrayed. Our relationship never recovered.

Here's another lesson I learned when becoming deeply involved with men in my congregation struggling with porn. The more I knew about an individual's struggle, the more that person felt apprehensive about coming to church. He could not help feeling uncomfortable when the guy preaching in front of 500 people on a Sunday morning knew so much about his private life. Eventually, he left the church I pastored. This happened more than once.

Counselors as Accountability Partners

Counselors offer a valuable service. They counsel. They help people hurting from their pasts learn to live in the present and build for the future. As emotional archeologists, they help people explore troubling pasts and find solutions for health and healing. By their very nature, they are not accountability partners. Most counselors I know refuse to accept this responsibility. It's simply outside what they ordinarily do.

Close Friends as Accountability Partners

This often strains a relationship. A close pastor friend of mine once asked me to suggest to him why his church struggled. It was extremely difficult for me to say to him the problem with his church was, well, himself. I suggested he hire an Executive Life Coach as I did not want to damage my relationship with him. Choosing to be his friend rather than an accountability partner was a wise decision. Be very careful here. Friends tend to be soft, letting you get by with too much. They tend to make excuses, or they get frustrated. Then the relationship falls apart, and the friendship drifts away. If you choose a friend for accountability, make sure he/she is up to the task.

Mature Christian Mentors

Chuck is a friend. He is in his fifties. He is the executive director of a small company in northern Minnesota. He is simply one of the best accountability partners and mentors of men I've ever seen. Most men Chuck works with do well. Chuck is passionate about helping men acquire the heart of Jesus and live pure lives.

Another friend comes to mind. His name is Marv. He is in his sixties and loves God, and he has an incredible heart for men. He is retired from the US Postal Service, and he probably knows more about the Bible than I do. He walks men through the Scripture and disciples them to live for Christ. His lovely wife serves women in the same manner. They are great assets to their church!

Find spiritually mature people like Chuck, Marv, and Karen in your church or circle of Christian influence. Find a church where such people exist! Search as diligently for them as you surf for porn on the Internet! God provides a way to escape temptation's clutches![90] It's there if you look for it.[91]

Life Coaches

I like the idea of a Life Coach. A trained, skilled, Christian Life Coach is an asset here. I've seen coaching work many, many times. As a Life Coach myself, it is my preferred method. A certified Christian Life Coach is a person trained with unique skill sets unlike anyone else. Coaches from organizations like Professional Christian Coaching Institute[92] are well-trained to coach people, helping them work through life's issues. However, a Life Coach most likely will not agree to become your accountability partner. What a Life Coach can do is help you discover within yourself good accountability. Solid accountability is probably right before your eyes. You just need a little help seeing it. In coaching, you will discover practical steps to successfully deal with pornography in your life.

Life Coaches charge for their services. Most guys think they should get those services for free, and they tend to resist. When I pressed Ben as to his reason for no longer seeing his coach he replied, "The guy wants 100 dollars per month!" Ben bellowed as he just recently moved into a cheap motel, separating from his wife, because of his porn. I replied, "What's the motel room costing you a month Ben?" Think, think, think, guys. If you want skilled professional help in this area, it will cost you. Prices range from $150 for two to three 45-minute sessions per month to up to $600 per month.

The sessions are often over the phone, and that provides a very safe way for a man to share his struggles. If the coach is ICF[93] or PCCI[94] certified, the Life Coach is bound to an ethic of confidentiality. You can find a life coach in your area.[95] And, in paying for the service, you can expect results! Too expensive you say? How much do you spend on porn? What's that costing you now, and what will it cost you in the future? What will it cost you in the end? Paying for a Life Coach increases resolve to overcome porn.

Parents

The temptations coming upon young men are overwhelming at times. My sons knew they could approach mom and dad without fear, judgment, or overreaction. Discuss it we did! They needed guidance and navigation in this area. That's not to say their parents became their sole or main source of accountability. We were one small piece of their armor. This is rare. Men who can talk with their fathers are quite fortunate to enjoy such a relationship. Moms willing to talk with their children and teens about the Internet and social media dangers are crucial, too. Many single moms I know do a great job discussing these issues with their children.

Accountability Partners and Pornography

Good accountability partners often struggled with and overcame pornography habits themselves. Some say they are the only ones who can truly understand the struggle and assist another. Perhaps that is true, but perhaps not.

During one of my pastorates, a number of men shared their "porn problems." Most had accountability partners. One particular man demonstrated the weakness of many accountability approaches. His accountability partner, another man, in his mid-30s, was recently fired from his job. He was dismissed when he was caught viewing porn on the company's computer, and, since this was his second dismissal for the same offense, he bemoaned his "bad luck."

A clear truth became apparent as I observed these two men. Another brother who is as weak or weaker cannot possibly provide accountability to ensure success for another person struggling with the same deficit. This type of accountability partner relationship often ends in complete shambles on many levels. Neither stands very long before returning to the dragon's dark dungeon. Choose your accountability partner carefully, with much prayer.

You as Your Own Best Accountability Partner

One question I ask men is, "How can you be accountable to yourself?" This befuddles most guys. They often reply with a shrug of their shoulders. I press them, asking, "How do you personally keep yourself accountable?"

Here are some practical suggestions for self-accountability:

1. **Picture your daughter in the porn images you are seeing.** This should disturb you. When you view porn, you are viewing the daughter or son of another father or mother being misused and abused. The problem with pornography is it's usually faceless to the viewer. When asked to describe women's faces in the porn

they view, most men return a blank stare. Pornography is a faceless, impersonal cyber encounter. Put your daughter's face in the mix. If you love your daughter more than you love yourself, picturing your daughter's face on the woman you're fantasizing about should jolt you back to reality. It's that sick. Someone's little girl is in that picture.

2. **If you don't have children.** Picture your sister's face on the face of that alluring woman.

3. **Or, picture your mom's face on the bodies of those young women, or even your grandma's face.** One guy told me, "If I think of my mom, that more than anything else kills my desire for pornography." He chuckled as he continued, "I suppose when it comes to sex, anytime anyone thinks of their parents that will just about kill any desire to have sex." We broke out in laughter together.

4. **For older men, I challenge, "Before you look at porn, Grandpa, think of your grandchildren.** Think of your granddaughter being lured into pornographic filming by some vile person. That's the reality, my friend." One older gentleman softly responded, "I can't think of porn if I'm thinking of my grandchildren." (Unfortunately, if you are into child porn, this probably will not work.)

5. **Understand Your Nature.** Know who you are. Know where you need to go. Many men in bondage to pornography confess a lack of ability to escape porn on their own. In Paul's letter to the Romans, he admits, "And I know that nothing good lives in me, that is, in my sinful nature. I want to do what is right, but I can't" (Romans 7:14).

6. **Own it.** Take full responsibility for your porn deficit. Whether you willingly ventured into pornography or became an ensnared victim, own your steps to freedom.

7. **Resolve to Overcome.** Until you make up your mind to deal with your problem, your problem will deal with you.

8. **Get to it!** Celebrate Recovery[96] is a great way to get started. There are thousands of chapters throughout the United States and in other countries, too. Take the initiative. Find a CR Recovery Group through their locator.[97] To get a feel for Celebrate Recovery's approach, study their twelve steps at:

https://www.celebraterecovery.com/index.php/about-us/twelve-steps

Key Essential

Ponder this question, "Do you really and truly wish to slay YOUR Porn Dragon? Do you really want to be free? Or will you continue believing you've got your little friend under control? That is, until you realize the little guy is now bigger than a six-story building in your life raining fire down upon you."

Find an accountability partner who lives above pornography. You need a lovingly tough and tenacious person who holds your feet to the fire. Find a partner who refuses to allow you to justify any time spent with your dragon. Find a partner who will, well, frankly, kick your butt every time you let your dragon out of its cage. Secure a partner who will not accept 80 percent obedience. Get someone who takes you to task when you are 20 percent disobedient. Anything less assures a continued failure.

You become the change needed in your life. Stop blaming your porn on everyone and everything else but yourself. Stop whining about how difficult porn is to overcome. Yes, you may believe yourself powerless to overcome, but those in Jesus Christ possess a greater power than pornography. "Greater is he that is in you, than he that is in the world" (1 John 4:4 KJV).

Understand where you are. **Own** your current situation. **Resolve** to take the necessary steps to overcome your deficit. **Get** to it! Take your first steps today. If these first steps prove too difficult for you, perhaps ask yourself this question, "Do I really, really want to kick this habit?" Only you can make the decision. The Bible promises, "For I can do everything through Christ, who gives me strength" (Philippians 4:13).

Scripture for Reflection

"For I can do everything through Christ, who gives me strength" (Philippians 4:13).

"As iron sharpens iron, so a friend sharpens a friend" (Proverbs 27:17).

Ponderings

1. What trespasses are you caught in? What are your secret sins?

2. What does your obedience look like? 100%, 90%, 80%, or less?

3. What do you think God's expectation of obedience in your life looks like?

4. Describe an ideal accountability partner.

5. Does your accountability partner live clearly above pornography?

6. Are you really and truly ready for your Porn Dragon to die?

7. What do you think of hiring a Life Coach to help you deal with your pornography?

8. What do you think about acquiring an older spiritual person to help?

9. What other ideas can you think about for accountability?

10. How will you develop accountability?

Prayer

Dear God,

Yes, I need a good accountability partner to help me deal with my dragon.

Please help me find the right person living above this problem,

A person who will hold me accountable in this battle.

A person who asks the tough questions, and provides the right answers.

Help me find that person who will speak truth to me.

A person I can call on in my times of temptation and trouble.

Most of all help me become the person who will take responsibility for my own change. Help me learn to honor you in all I do.

So Be It! – Amen.

CHAPTER 8

CONFESSION

"A sinning man stops praying, a praying man stops sinning."
Leonard Ravenhill

"But if we confess our sins to him, he is faithful and just to forgive us our sins and to cleanse us from all wickedness."
1 John 1:9

"Confess your sins to each other and pray for each other so that you may be healed. The earnest prayer of a righteous person has great power and produces wonderful results."
James 5:16

"People who conceal their sins will not prosper, but if they confess and turn from them, they will receive mercy."
Proverbs 28:13

"If I had not confessed the sin in my heart, the Lord would not have listened."
Psalms 66:18

Finally, I confessed all my sins to you and stopped trying to hide my guilt. I said to myself, "I will confess my rebellion to the Lord." And you forgave me! All my guilt is gone.
Psalm 32:5

While trying to assist a young man struggling with porn, I listened as he confessed, "Dear God, I'm sorry about looking at the Internet again. I know it's not a good thing. Help me to do better. Amen."

I looked straight into his eyes and said, "Is this perhaps one reason you're not getting victory over this in your life right now?"

"What do you mean?" he shot back.

I said, "That's really not a confession. It's pretty weak. If you really want to be rid of this thing, the secret is in confession. Confession must be patterned after the Bible. Can I show you what confession really looks like?" With that, we began.

King David, the second king of ancient Israel and author of many of the Psalms, wrote Psalms 32 and 51. The Book of Psalms is a collection of lyric poems, originally set to music, and each is a prayer, thought, or meditation. Psalms 32 and 51 are part of a collection of seven repentance Psalms.[98] We believe King David wrote these two Psalms after committing horrible atrocities that sprang from sexual sin. **Read these two Psalms. Meditate upon them.** Study David's fall, confrontation, suffering, punishment, discipline, confession, and restoration. David's transparent confession bares his soul to us. His story is recorded that we might learn, and not fall into the same errors.[99] Let's look at the story a bit.

It was the golden age of Israel, and among the prominent men of the day was Uriah, known as one of David's Mighty Men.[100] Uriah was an elite warrior, and he was famous for his exploits. King David is in the middle of dealing with a serious issue threatening to tarnish his reputation. He hoped Uriah might help him deal with a complication that might imperil his reign. But we need to go back a little further to see the irony in the situation.

According to the narrative in 2 Samuel 11, on one of Jerusalem's balmy evenings, David took a walk upon the roof of his palace, a flat hard roof common in the Middle East. I've sat on several such roofs in Israel, India, and even Haiti. These roofs are wonderful places to escape the heat of the day and unwind. During a recent trip to Haiti, my son and I sat together on a flat concrete roof every evening under the stars conversing and sharing with each other. It was a highlight of my trip!

Whatever David's reason, he found himself walking on his roof one evening. Down below, this night, something caught his eye. Something beautiful, young, and intriguing made this moment different from all others. Down below his rooftop level, a very attractive young woman named Bathsheba was bathing.

Bathsheba was the granddaughter of Ahithophel, one of David's most trusted counselors. Here, in the early evening hours, Bathsheba washed. David noticed her. Having studied this passage repeatedly, I am convinced David's seeing of Bathsheba was a casual circumstance. He did not plan this event. It unfolded in front of his eyes. His decisions after the initial glance scarred his reign, family, friends, and kingdom for the rest of his life.

After seeing Bathsheba, he wanted to know who she was. Most English translations of the Bible say, "He sent messengers *to fetch* her." Some sources try to place most of the blame for this encounter on Bathsheba, portraying her as a seductive temptress trying to lure a strolling king into a sexual liaison. David was simply a man, according to that narrative, who couldn't resist the sexual seductions of this young woman. It is interesting how 3,000 years later that excuse and lie is still used today by so many men.

A closer look at the narrative reveals something quite different.

A study in the original language of the passage seems to indicate something far more sinister on David's part. And, it places the sole blame in David's corner. Richard M. Davidson in *Journal of Adventist Theology* notes:

> David "takes her" and he "lies with her." The word *laqach* ["take"] in this context (of sending royal messengers) should probably be understood in the sense of "fetch" (NJB) or "summon" and clearly implies psychological power pressure on the part of David and not voluntary collusion on the part of Bathsheba. According to the text, David sends "messengers" (plural), but the verb *laqach* ["take"] has a singular masculine subject ("he took her").[101]

David's "taking" of Bathsheba indicated who was in control. David's fetching and bringing her into his bedchambers indicated power. David, the ancient king, held absolute power. Once in his palace, how would Bathsheba dare to stand up to a King? People lost their lives for much less in ancient days. Once in the king's bedchamber, though, one might hear the cries of a young Bathsheba, who would dare to intervene? To somehow soften David's sin here, the power question is largely ignored. But, it appears that David used his power to rape Bathsheba. Ahithophel's desertion of David, some years later, when David's son Absalom rebelled, may indicate this as true.[102] Ahithophel was Bathsheba's grandfather. Years later, when Ahithophel responded negatively to David in crisis, that response appears to corroborate the rape of a very young Bathsheba.

How does a king cover up his rape of the wife of a trusted military hero? How does he contain the story and keep it from spreading through his palace? How does one prevent it leaking into the community? David had a plan.

Upon learning Bathsheba was pregnant, David summoned Uriah from the front lines of battle back to Jerusalem. While engaging in friendly chitchat, grandstanding, and posturing, David encouraged Uriah to take his leave to go to his home and wife. Uriah refused. This refusal eventually cost him his life.

Uriah may have already heard what took place with the king. He also appeared to hold to a common code of valor among Israel's warriors. Abstinence from sex during military engagements assured focus upon the battle at hand. Uriah stated this to David during their conversation. Spending time with his wife while the entire army of Israel was on the front lines engaged in battle was not honorable in his view.

David tried to weaken Uriah through strong drink and then ordered him to his home. David desperately ordered, "You go home and have sex with your wife!" He needed Uriah to sleep with his wife Bathsheba so that Uriah, rather than David, would appear to be the father of the coming child. In David's covering of his guilt, he attempted to hide his sexual sin. Does any of this sound familiar?

Rather than go in to his wife, Uriah spent the night on his front porch. Uriah's refusal marked integrity among soldiers at war in ancient days. In battle, a warrior did not leave the front line for familial pleasures. Not even if a king commanded it. Hearing of Uriah's stubbornness and tenacity, David sent Uriah back to his unit on the front lines. Without his knowledge, he carried his own death warrant from his king. Handing the orders to his commander, Joab, Uriah was placed on the very front lines of battle the next day. As the battle heated up, Joab, by order of David, pulled back most of his troops leaving Uriah exposed. Uriah died in battle that day, murdered by his own king and sent to his death by his own general.

Upon hearing the news, David, the "gracious, compassionate, King" took the poor unfortunate widow, Bathsheba, into his home making her a member of the royal family. David's son would be born into a legitimate family. They would all live happily ever after—or so David thought.

One day, David, in his majestic robes, sat on his royal throne conducting the business of a king. A visitor approached the royal court. The revered old prophet Nathan presented himself. With the royal scribes, servants, and other officials present Nathan, the aged prophet, begins to tell the king a story.

"Oh, king," he began, "There was a poor man who possessed only one little ewe lamb. He was very poor, but he loved that one little lamb. He cherished his little lamb deeply providing for its every need. The lamb ate from his table. He cherished the little lamb like a young daughter. (Note, this would reflect Bathsheba's youthfulness). Next to him lived a very wealthy man. The rich man possessed many head of cattle, lambs, and wealth. This wealthy man saw the poor man's little beautiful ewe lamb. The rich man liked what he saw. One day a guest arrived at the rich man's house, but instead of killing one of his own sheep to prepare a meal for his guest, he took the poor man's young lamb, killed it, prepared it, and presented it to his guest."

As these words fell from Nathan's mouth, David exploded into hypocritical, self-righteous anger. He denounced the rich man and made a heated proclamation. David vowed, "He will pay back for all he took four times over!"

Those words had barely left David's mouth when the old prophet pointed his finger at David and said, "David! You are that man! And, you will pay for this sin. You've already pronounced your own sentence."

Immediately David crumbled and confessed his sin. He did not deny. He did not waffle. He was guilty, and he knew it. He admitted it. David's house experienced bloody turmoil from this moment on till the end of his life.[103]

Now, while David's act seems sexual in nature, there is so much more going on, deeper and darker. It's an extreme example of where sexual lust takes a man. You most likely are not anywhere close to David's situation. Let's hope not. The pain, damage, and death were a nightmare for David! Fortunately, for David, he awoke, and the nightmare ended, at least in part. There is a good ending to David's story—well, let's say a restored ending. Hopefully, it gives you hope in your story wherever you find yourself today.

The amazing part of this story, to me, is David's confessions recorded in the Psalms. His confessions, are honest, transparent, and sincere. As the story unfolded, it intensifies. God's forgiveness, removal of David's guilt, and restoration left rational, logical people asking, "How can this be?"

How can such offenses be forgiven? God is incredible, His mercy beyond comprehension. Forgiveness does not eliminate all of sin's ramifications. David's actions shadowed him the rest of his life. Some people injured by his actions struggled to forgive him. Note Ahithophel's desertion sometime later. Domestic violence plagued David's family. Yet, in all this, God forgave and restored. The key is in David's confession of his sin. He lived serving God and his people successfully despite his sin. God's grace is often a paradox—a contradiction of the human experience. Confession was the process that cleansed and delivered David. In David's confession, there is a transformational model for our confession. Here is the key to healing, mending, and deliverance. Read David's confession in Psalm 32:

Oh, what joy for those whose disobedience is forgiven, whose sin is put out of sight! Yes, what joy for those whose record the Lord has cleared of guilt, whose lives are lived in complete honesty! When I refused to confess my sin, my body wasted away, and I groaned all day long. Day and night your hand of discipline was heavy on me. My strength evaporated like water in the summer heat.

Finally, I confessed all my sins to you and stopped trying to hide my guilt. I said to myself, "I will confess my rebellion to the Lord." And you forgave me! All my guilt is gone.

Therefore, let all the godly pray to you while there is still time, that they may not drown in the floodwaters of judgment. For you are my hiding place; you protect me from trouble. You surround me with songs of victory.

The Lord says, "I will guide you along the best pathway for your life. I will advise you and watch over you. Do not be like a senseless horse or mule that needs a bit and bridle to keep it under control."

Notice the components here. Try to get a good hold on this chapter. Experience the devastation, and compare it with the joy and restoration offered. Understand David's depth of sin. Look at the man David, the depravity of his offenses, and the limitless love of God's restoring grace. See God's vast expanse of grace enveloping David in an awful condition. Embrace the promises in this chapter, and the pathway to hope and restoration.

Forgiveness Yields Joy

"Oh, the joy of those whose sin or disobedience is forgiven." David repeated this phrase in verse two. He declared in another Psalm, "For his anger lasts only a moment, but his favor lasts a lifetime! Weeping may last through the night, but joy comes with the morning" (Psalm 30:5). This verse is often quoted at funerals, but it is not a verse about physical death. It speaks of renewal.

Experiencing God's forgiveness brings a refreshing renewal of our lives. David, despite his twisted behavior, received undeserved forgiveness, renewal, and restoration. Is it any wonder David so ecstatically credited God for the good things in his life?

Know this, my friend, regardless of your current struggles, God in His grace is there. God's grace is greater than any blot or blemish you carry today. God's grace is faithful. And God makes his grace freely accessible and available to you, right this very moment. Regardless of your dragon's fury, God's grace is more powerful. No matter how you view yourself right now, or other people for that matter, God's joyful, merciful, unending, boundless, magnificent grace is available for you right this very moment! He can and will renew you if you meet God on His terms. If you model David's confession in sincerity, joy is yours. It's up to you. Joy is restoration's ultimate aim. An old hymn says, "There is joy unspeakable and full of glory …" It's joy so full of jubilation that any attempt to describe it falls short.

Action

In the first two verses, three terms are used to describe David's confessional actions: disobedience, sin, and guilt. Let's break each of these words down a bit.

Disobedience: David stated that his sin was first and foremost directed at God. David's actions were contrary to God's best plans for his life. His actions negatively impacted God's best intentions for both Bathsheba and Uriah. David's sin harmed numerous people, but first and foremost they assaulted the very integrity of God. David admitted this. The word "disobedience" in the Hebrew language is much stronger than our English translation. It carries a heavy weight of, "rebellion, transgression, or a breach of trust." David breached God's trust in him, and that of so many others.

Sin: This word in the original language carries the idea of a sacrifice or sin offering required to cleanse David from his offense. Payment was required. David's ability to make full payment for his debt of his offenses was impossible. Full restoration depended upon God. God made a way to deal with David's sin, not only punishing him but restoring David back to a relationship with Himself.

Guilt: The Hebrew word, *avon* is used more than 200 times in the Old Testament. Its root meaning carries the thought of perversity, depravity, and iniquity. It has the idea of being crooked, perverse, twisted, and evildoing. David described his actions as twisted and perverted. This weighty word suggests David's activity was criminal in nature. It is a strong, accurate, and sobering description of his sin. David held nothing back. He didn't gloss anything over. No rationalizing. No blame shifting. No excuses. David understood the gravity of his sin. In Psalm 51, there is another confession for this incident. David described his guilt further in descriptive terms, "Stain of my sins, from my guilt, my sin, my rebellion, done what is evil in your sight, and shedding of blood."

Confession's first step is to see the gravity of your sin.

Understand the severity of your actions. See sin's ugliness. Smell the stench. See sin from God's perspective. Understanding sin from God's viewpoint gives a meta view of sin. It shows how personal sin affects so much more than just the individual committing sin. It lays waste to the argument, "As long as I'm not hurting anyone it's okay."

David cried out in Psalms 51:4, "Against you, and you alone, have I sinned; I have done what is evil in your sight." Grasp that. A raped woman, a murdered man, a dishonored palace, a defeat in battle, a shamed country, schemes, betrayal and lies—and yet David maintained that his greatest offense was against God and God only.

Here is the foundation upon which effective confession is built. If you truly desire to experience God's forgiveness and deliverance, see pornography the way God does. It is an affront against a loving Creator.

To Confess or Not to Confess

Among men dealing with porn, confession is pathetically weak or nonexistent. It's not that these struggling men's lives are prayerless. Oh, they pray! Men beg for help and mercy all the time. They just rarely confess the depth and depravity of their sin to a loving, caring, heavenly Father. Often, in embarrassment, they fear to mention their shameful deeds to themselves and God.

Confessionless living has negative consequences on a person's health. David talked about "wasting away" and "groaning" all day long. The idea is literally that of growing old before one's time or to be completely used up. Unconfessed sin will eat you alive, bringing about undesirable side effects. Perhaps the worst consequence of unconfessed sin is you'll not realize the process of degradation taking place within you and around you.

Then, David described God's heavy hand of discipline upon him. In Psalm 51, he said that he was broken. God's discipline of His people sets a recurring theme throughout the entire Bible. Simply put, if you belong to God, He cares about you. He disciplines those He loves. He reserves the right as Creator to discipline you as heavily and severely as needed to get you back on track; His track. Scripture teaches God disciplines those He truly loves.[104] If you are under the heavy hand of God's discipline, it's because He's trying to bring you to the point of confession. David described God's discipline upon him as harsh. It literally sapped his strength. He lamented, "My strength evaporated like water in the summer heat …" The image is of a person fainting from sunstroke. In David's unconfessed state, he fainted in the heat of God's discipline upon his life.

Next, the mental and emotional turmoil of living in such a state became unbearable. In Psalm 51 David said, "For I recognize my rebellion; it haunts me day and night." David lived as a haunted man hiding his secret life. Often men describe their pornographic lives as nightmares. One man desperately cried, "It's like my life is a haunted house. Everywhere I turn, stuff keeps popping up."

Imagine King David sitting on his throne doing what ancient kings did in that day. One day he's judging an offense between quarreling parties. "Oh, great king, I caught this man with my wife, and now I ask for restitution for his sins," is just one possibility. Or, "Mighty great king, this man stole my cattle and rebranded them to make it appear that they belonged to him. I ask for justice oh, king." Think of the incredible pain in David's life living in such self-deceptive hypocrisy.

David reached a breaking point, "Finally, I confessed all my sins to you and stopped trying to hide my guilt."

Notice the elements of his confession:

1. "Finally" – there comes the point when one can only turn to God for healing and wholeness. From the moment Uriah died in battle until Nathan the prophet confronted David before his throne that day, David suffered immensely. Much misfortune had occurred. A baby was born to Bathsheba. David's child survived perhaps a year, meaning David hid his sin nearly two full years. Nathan confronted David. Finally, David could hide no longer. He broke under his sin. David was caught red-handed and confronted before everyone. The weight of his guilt overwhelmed him. Brokenness is painful. Brokenness is humbling. Brokenness brings soul wrenching. Yet, brokenness is necessary.

2. "All my sins" – He took inventory of his twisted actions. There was no whitewashing here. No blame shifting. No rationalization. No personal victimization. No, "Well, God, you see... it was a hot night, and I accidentally saw Bathsheba's, naked body while walking on the balcony of my palace, and well, I, I, I guess ... well, Lord you understand, a hot night, a beautiful woman, and a man, a king, well, and besides there is a lot of pressure on being a king, and my 50 other wives, and 70 other mistresses, well, they just weren't meeting my needs, God. I needed to unwind, and well ... hey God, anything can happen on a hot night on the roof." None of that! David finally rid himself of the lies and deception! He stopped lying to himself, to his family, and to the nation. Holding nothing back, hiding nothing, David finally came clean, admitting all. He began naming his sins one by one. There was no softening of his transgressions. This was confession. No pretense. No lightening of the crime. No projecting it upon someone else, something else, or some course of events. "God, I am guilty ..." is all David could say.

3. "Stopped trying to hide" – This pattern is typical of guilty people. Remember when Adam and Eve sinned in the Garden of Eden? What did they do? They went and hid.[105] Remember when Cain killed his brother Abel? What did he do? He ran away and hid from God.[106] Remember when Jonah, the Old Testament prophet, refused to obey God? What did he do? He went the opposite direction from Nineveh, and tried to hide in a boat.[107] Achan sinned and hid from God, too.[108] Remember when Peter denied he knew Jesus? He denied him three times using foul language.[109] Remember what he did immediately afterward? He went and hid. Ever since Adam's sin, the guilty have tried to hide from their sin.

4. "Hide my guilt" – David finally saw the only way was to come clean before a just and holy God. Naming his sin, he hid nothing. His twisted actions were brought to light. He finally understood the saying in the Book of Proverbs, "God is everywhere in every place beholding both good and evil."[110]

5. "Confess Rebellion to the Lord" – What did David actually confess? What was his greatest guilt? Of all the things he might mention, he cited only one, what he considered his greatest sin. He declared, "I will confess my rebellion to the LORD." Why did he not say, "Forgive me for what I did to Uriah? Forgive me for the lies. Sorry for getting Bathsheba pregnant." No. He centered upon his ultimate offense. All sin is ultimately directed towards God.

After David's confession, positive things happened. Notice:

1. "You forgave me!" – Imagine! Despite all David did—all his wrong, all his evil deeds, and all his crooked actions—God forgave him. God cleared his slate. His sin was covered. People sometimes ask, "What about Uriah? How does that help him? He seems to get the raw end of the deal here, doesn't he?" The Bible indicates a heavenly reckoning will take place one day when all things are made right. Faithfulness will be rewarded. Injustices will be compensated. In some eternal way, God will set everything right.[111] For now, David was cleared! He was freed from the heaviness of guilt, and he could sing, "My sins are gone! I'm forgiven! I'm restored! I can talk freely again! Free, free, free!"

2. **"My guilt is gone!"** – In South Africa, I owned several handguns, necessary for protection in a violent society. One day when we moved into a new home, one of my handguns was stolen. Ironically, that made me guilty of a crime under South Africa law. I filed a report with the police and secured a lawyer. Securing my handguns was my responsibility. My lawyer represented me before a South African magistrate or judge. The judge looked at me and said, "Mr. Mingo you are clearly negligent here and guilty. However, since you declared the theft of your weapon in an appropriate way immediately, this court suspends your sentence." Being declared forgiven by the judge was both freeing and relieving. There was a sigh of relief! My guilt was gone! My slate was clean! Imagine if had I chosen to hide my guilt, and not report my crime. What might the consequences be if the gun turned up in the hands of some felon a year or two later?

3. **"Let the godly pray while there is still time ..."** – David urged godly people to confess their sins, before sin's weight and damage was beyond human remedy. Notice David's description of people involved in this type of confession—they are "godly." Living above or better than everyone else in the church is not necessarily

the high mark of godliness. A mark of godly quality is confession of personal sin. Before the full effects of sin and God's discipline bears down upon the guilty, David urged confession. Confession bares many great results. A forgiven David declared:

- God is my hiding place
- God protects in time of trouble
- God surrounds me with songs of victory
- God guides me along the best path for my life
- God advises me
- God watches over me
- God protects me from trouble
- God's unfailing love protects me
- God purifies my heart
- God gives me joy and happiness

4. A broken and repentant spirit is the goal – David clearly showed that apart from confession, nothing else was acceptable to God. Nothing. He said, "You do not desire a sacrifice, or I would offer one. You do not want a burnt offering. The sacrifice you desire is a broken spirit. You will not reject a broken and repentant heart, O God."[112]

Key Essentials

Confession of sin is essential in overcoming pornographic habits. Naming a sin for what it truly is before an ever-present God brings sin out into the open. Understanding the awful weight of pornography before a holy and graceful God produces brokenness and repentance. Confessing porn's damage to others is essential, too. Porn is never a secret sin. Most of all, porn distracts you from God. We were created in His image.[113] We were created in resemblance to God. Porn opposes the very image of a loving, caring God. Confession acknowledges this. Confession declares porn as not only a sin against one's self, but sin against so many others. In confession of tainting God's image of Himself in us, it purges us from all these aversions.[114]

Scripture for Reflection

"Confess your sins to each other and pray for each other so that you may be healed. The earnest prayer of a righteous person has great power and produces wonderful results" (James 5:16).

"On the other hand, if we admit our sins—make a clean breast of them—he won't let us down; he'll be true to himself. He'll forgive our sins and purge us of all wrongdoing" (1 John 1:9 MSG).

Ponderings

1. Define confession.
2. Describe your confessional life.
3. How do you confess your sin?
4. To whom do you confess your sin?
5. How do you confess, in particular, your porn sin?
6. What do you think about David's sins?
7. How do you think Nathan's confrontation helped David confess his sins?
8. What do you think about David's restoration in the light of the devastating effects his actions had on so many others?
9. Do you think it fair that God restored David? Why did God restore David?

10. What were the lasting results of David's actions?

11. What does God's Grace look like here?

12. Can God do the same for you as He did for David?

Prayer

God,

I confess that I have viewed people created in your image for selfish sexual excitement. My pornography viewing violates your nature and your creation.

Pornography lies.

It's not beautiful.

It's not safe.

It's not harmless.

It's not okay.

You are a caring, loving God who created us, me, to resemble who You are. Pornography sullies this image.

When I sin, it violates your very nature. It harms your creation.

I confess this sin to you.

It is against you that I have sinned. God forgive me for the harm I either knowingly or unknowingly caused to others. And, forgive me for what I've done to myself, your creation.

Show me your mercy.

Create a clean heart in me.

Give me a right spirit.

Restore to me the joy of seeing other people as you created them.

Lead me in your way.

So Be It – Amen.

CHAPTER 9

KNOWLEDGE

"The fear of the Lord is the beginning of knowledge;
fools despise wisdom and instruction."
Proverbs 1:7

"For wisdom will come into your heart, and
knowledge will be pleasant to your soul;"
Proverbs 2:10

"Intelligent people are always ready to learn. Their
ears are open for knowledge."
Proverbs 18:15

"We are all born ignorant, but one must work hard
to remain stupid."
Benjamin Franklin

This Knowledge technique is something I developed over years of trying to help men slay their Porn Dragons. Asking a series of pointed, tough, personal questions helps them see where pornography wants to take them. It demonstrates how pornography wants to destroy their lives and the lives of those around them. We learn how pornography is destroying the lives of those who willingly give themselves to it, and to those forced into sex slavery because of it. This experience is direct, plain, blunt, revealing, painful, assaulting, and sobering.

Know Porn Road's End

Have you ever asked yourself, "What's the end of this road I am on?" While I was writing this book, a former church member messaged me about someone we both knew.

When I was interviewing for the Senior Pastor position at his church nine years ago, the call committee and chairman elder assured me that the church was in great shape, ready for a leader of my caliber to "lead us to the next step." In complete naivety, I accepted the call and tried to settle into American life and ministry after years of living in Africa.

Within months, I sensed "something is wrong here." First, there were several hundred thousand dollars unaccounted for on the books. When I asked about receipts and financial records, I was told: "none existed." No one seemed to know quite for sure where the receipts went. Requests for an audit went unaddressed.

Something else began to emerge. Something darker lurked within the corners of that congregation. Within that group of wonderful people existed a handful of men, past and present leaders, living lies of sullied self-delusion.

Before my arrival, one man held the position of chairman elder at this church. Very influential, he claimed to be the only elder besides the Senior Pastor on the board during his tenure. I wondered what happened to the rest of those elders. When did they leave the board? What were the circumstances? He often declared, "Before you came, it was just me and pastor. Just the two of us made all the decisions."

Red flags went up.

First, he was extremely controlling in his home. His wife couldn't breathe without his dominant presence insisting on knowing every detail of her daily activity. He seemed to suffocate his daughters' personalities, too. Every detail of their activities—all their movements, the people they spoke with, everything—required explanation. After getting to know his daughters a bit, my wife said more than once to me, "That guy gives me the creeps. Something is going on there."

The message I had received from the former church member asked, "Did you hear about _____?" As I was writing these very lines, I was looking at a photograph on the Minnesota Department of Corrections Offender Locator Link website. There he was, that elder. Next to his mug shot on my phone screen were some details. I saw he was sentenced for one count of second-degree sexual criminal conduct against each of his three daughters. Today, he resides in a Minnesota Corrections Facility.

Some of his criminal acts took place during his tenure in church leadership. I seem to recall that during our elders' prayer times he always asked prayer for his oldest daughter who was "drifting away from God and the church." I'll say.

Would you care to guess where this all started? Pornography. Many years prior, what began as his taking a quick glance at nudity and sexual activity progressed to hardcore sexual misconduct and criminal activity—activity far beyond anything this dad ever imaged or anticipated. Never in his wildest, deepest, darkest thinking did he ever picture himself in prison for sexually assaulting his daughters.

He has learned a hard lesson and now faces a bleak future in prison. His once well rounded, smiling face is gaunt, angry, and scared. And even more tragic are the injuries inflicted upon his daughters by their trusted father in the innocence of their adolescence.

It was painfully interesting to learn that the Senior Pastor, prior to my accepting a pastoral call at the church, "struggled" with pornography. His son broke that news to the congregation, during a morning service, announcing his father's bondage, to everyone in the congregation. That little piece of information was never mentioned during my interview. Was it any wonder, the men on the board of elders refused to discipline another church member when he announced to his wife an open marriage arrangement. He would now spend the weekends with his wife and children, but Monday through Thursday he'd stay with his new girlfriend across town. This was known to everyone in that town, and finally culminated when a business person pressed me, "Hey, what are you guys doing over there at your church? How can you just ignore this?" Unable to act, or should I say, not permitted to discipline the individual, my resignation followed shortly after. Failing to discipline ruined the testimony of that church and much more.

Know Porn Kills Intimacy

Dr. Williams M. Struthers, PhD, Associate Professor of Psychology at Wheaton College, warns of the dangers constant pornography viewing has on rewiring the brain. In his article, "The Effects of Porn on the Male Brain," he discusses five chemicals produced in the brain when a person indulges in regular, repeated viewing of pornography. [115] These chemicals alter the brain to such a degree that actual intimate sex is no longer arousing. The constant production of dopamine and other chemicals in the brain drastically alters the parts of the brain in control of a man's response to sexual stimulation. Ironically, through repeated porn exposure many men lose the ability to relate sexually.

ASAP Science produced a video called *The Science of Porn Addiction*.[116] According to the video, porn changes the brain radically, much like an addiction. This addiction produces compulsive and addictive sexual behaviors, and among them, withdrawal from intimacy is a common occurrence. Through repeated production of dopamine caused by porn exposure, a normal, fulfilling sexual relationship becomes uninteresting.[117]

Know Porn Numbs and Deadens

Your Porn Dragon seeks to take you down into the depths of sexual debauchery, far beyond your wildest intention. When finished, it will lead you into cesspools of numbness beyond your darkest imagination. Ultimately your dragon will slay you in the sewer of debauchery. At that point, you will realize that it was no friend at all. Initially appearing as a friend, your Porn Dragon reveals itself as The Destroyer. The price paid for this deception is higher than anything envisaged.[118]

Or to change the metaphor, think of how an outhouse smells. The smell, while at first offensive, will not bother you as much over time. Porn works like that. In fact, you will reach a point that nothing smells or appears abnormal in your broken world. As the Porn Dragon gains strength and grows larger than life, nothing will quench or satisfy the fire of its demands.

Worst of all, the Porn Dragon produces spiritual leprosy. Leprosy is a disease that deadens the nerves until one can't sense touch any longer. Repeated injuries damage the skin and limbs because there is little sensitivity to pain.[119] Leprosy sufferers' injuries are often self-inflicted as they simply can't sense the damage caused through blunt contact with objects. I witnessed this in Africa.

Men who are spending large amounts of time viewing pornography often complain of many side effects. They lack interest in sexual contact with their spouses. Their ability for sexual arousal erodes, and this leads to other problems. In *GQ* magazine, an article by Scott Christian, "10 Reason Why You Should Quit Watching Porn," discusses the findings of a Reddit community committed to abstaining from porn and masturbation. The results of the study are quite sobering,[120] as participants reported several downsides to porn watching, including some of the problems listed in this section.

Author Naomi Wolf in her Huffington Post article, "The Dangers of Porn Addiction and the 'Kink Spiral'" charges, "Porn is addicting and desensitizing. What it does to men over time—and I'm not making a moral judgment—is that it makes them less attracted to their partner. They're literally neuro-biologically bonding with the porn rather than their partner."[121] Naomi Wolf, an acknowledged feminist, sounds the alarm. It is not just the Church and Christians talking here.

Know Your Possible Porn End

The porn path you're traveling leads to your destruction and that of many of those around you. This habit is also expensive, leading many families to financial ruin. Talking about such a lifestyle, Solomon, the "wisest of all kings," once noted, "For a prostitute will bring you to poverty."[122] He was talking about a man who lives life only for sexual promiscuity. Promiscuity always leads to dire consequences. He finished the verse by saying, "But sleeping with another man's wife will cost you your life." The Bible, though written thousands of years ago, shows the end of such a lifestyle, by warning everyone traveling this road, "There is a path before each person that seems right, but it ends in death." [123] Many men fail to realize such consequences.

While pastoring in the Twin Cities, the news came to me that another pastor had fallen into sin. This pastor had enjoyed success, pastoring one of the larger churches in the area. He was a gifted speaker and communicator. Though he appeared to be at the top of his game, a three-year affair with his personal assistant ended his ministry and marriage. A friend of mine in the area knew this pastor, and he told me, "He is really struggling. His wife divorced him. He's living in Florida, and can barely make ends meet, selling used cars." Would you care to guess where this former pastor's downward slide began? A paraphrasing of that Proverb answers the question: "By means of a pornographic lifestyle a man is brought to only a piece of bread."

Know the Man You Are Becoming

When I was a pastor, occasionally, level-three sex offenders attended our church services. They were required by state law to report their status. Usually, a call to their respective parole officers was required. The conditions of the individual's parole determined the level of participation at our church. Most were not allowed near children.

For this reason, in one church I pastored, all children's ministries were moved to the West side of the facility, while all adult activities took place on the East side of the building. We thoroughly screened, checked the background, and trained any adult working with children. Some long-term members did not care for the new safety measures. My answer to them was always, "The measures we put into place are not because of you. It's to ensure that that one icky person does not injure any of our children."

As I talked with many of these sex offenders, the enormous cost of porn was sadly evident. Some, once high-income professionals, now lived with meager resources. Many were barren, lonely, bitter men. Some are listed in a predator's registry known to everyone in the community. As one formerly successful man said, "What I did cost me everything—my marriage, my family, my job, and my integrity. No one wants to be near me now. But, Don, you know what? I can't stop. I wish I'd never have started in the first place."

Take a long look at yourself in the mirror. Is this the kind of person you wish to become? No? Then, know it, understand it, own it, deal with it, and turn from it. Get hold of it before it gets a hold on you. What kind of person are you becoming?

Know Porn Viewing Contributes to Worldwide Sex Trafficking and Sexual Abuse[124]

When you click, you help put another child or woman into sex trafficking slavery. Demand drives the need for supply. The click helps drive greater demand. The supply is partly provided through ever increasing worldwide sex trafficking.

There is plenty of evidence for this. Many participants of graphic pornographic filming are forced, participants. Most pornography is not as glamorous and mutually enjoyable as portrayed. Women are often unwillingly forced into degrading, harsh, and painful sexual acts for profit and financial gain.

The Office of Juvenile Justice and Delinquency Prevention (OJJDP), estimates that more than 200,000 children are sexually exploited annually in the United States alone. The most common forms of commercial sexual exploitation of children are sex trafficking, child pornography, and child sex tourism (per Women's Support Project 2014).[125] That young, adult-looking woman you're watching on the Internet may be, in fact, someone's kidnapped, underage little girl.

Financial incentives for making pornography help to explain the production of over 11,000 adult films Hollywood releases every year.[126] The simple fact of the matter is that men's unbridled lust drives most of the pornographic industry. Halting demand, and thus the flow of money, would greatly curtail pornographic enterprises.

In 2011, two Miami men were found guilty of luring women into a sex trafficking trap for over five years. Advertising that they were auditioning new models, they lured young women to auditions, drugged them, kidnapped them, raped them, and videotaped the acts. They sold the videos to pornography stores and businesses across the country. And this is just one case of hundreds. Sex traffickers know that porn presents great opportunities to profit from their victims."[127] One source says that "owning" just four children for sex trafficking could help you earn more than $600,000 per year.[128]

Donna M. Hughes drafted a resolution and submitted it through the *Coalition Against Trafficking in Women to the United Nations Working Group on Contemporary Forms of Slavery,* Geneva, Switzerland. Back in 1998, she sounded the alarm:

Pimps actually drive the World Wide Web![129] "The movement of the sex industry to the Internet has increased the demand for new and more extreme images of the sexual exploitation of women and children. Older images identified by color quality of the image or clothing and hairstyle are viewed with disdain. Buyers demand new images with the scenes of sexual exploitation and abuse that are in fashion among predators. The result is increased abuse and exploitation of women and children."[130] Web pornographers are the most innovative entrepreneurs on the Internet."[131]

Know Your Viewing of Porn Helps Drive the Exploitation of Women and Children

When **you** view porn, **you** are one of the reasons porn exists. You create that demand. Every time a computer clicks to a porn site, it increases the demand for porn, thereby increasing the need for participants to produce porn. This demand fuels supply. Supply subjugates women and children to horrible, life-destroying sexual abuse. That is what your porn viewing encourages. You really are never alone and in secret. "As long as it doesn't hurt anyone else," never applies. Porn viewing promotes slavery. Is that sobering? Learn, acquire knowledge, and make better decisions.

A new phenomenon has arisen. There is a Dark Net used by tens of thousands of predators, pedophiles, and perverts. They swap images of children being sexually exploited. Britain's National Crime Agency warned in its 2014 threat assessment that abusers were turning to anonymous sites and encryption technology. The Dark Net is used to refer to parts of the internet that are hidden and hard to access without special software.[132]

New technology allows people to use TOR or "onion-routing," making a computer's net address extremely difficult to detect. US investigators say the amount of child abuse imagery on the net is growing rapidly.[133]

Use creates demand. Every click, your click, my click, is just one click away from helping enslave a child, young person, or woman into a horrible life of exploitation and trauma. Know the consequences of internet porn. Make an informed decision to change your behavior. Right now. This very moment. Today.

Know Porn Separates You From God, Your Family, and Yourself

One of the most arresting verses in the Bible says, "It's your sins that have cut you off from God. Because of your sins, he has turned away and will not listen anymore" (Isaiah 59:2). This is why God hates sin. Sin is the opposite of who God is. "So we are lying if we say we have fellowship with God but go on living in spiritual darkness; we are not practicing the truth" (1 John 1:6). Therefore confession is so important. Just three verses later John proclaims, "But if we confess our sins to him, he is faithful and just to forgive us our sins and to cleanse us from all wickedness." Sometimes men in porn don't see porn as a real sin. John addresses that, too: "If we claim we have no sin, we are only fooling ourselves and not living in the truth" (1 John 1:9). Why did John write these words? He declares his reason, "that you may fully share our joy" (1 John 1:4).

Key Essentials

Taking a long, sobering look at the multiple layers of harm pornography causes is crucial. Understanding exactly what you do every time pornography is accessed uncovers its consequences. Know you never win against pornography while living in pornography. There is never a good outcome as long as Your Porn Dragon is a companion.

Scripture for Reflection

"So we are lying if we say we have fellowship with God but go on living in spiritual darkness; we are not practicing the truth. But if we are living in the light, as God is in the light, then we have fellowship with each other, and the blood of Jesus, his Son, cleanses us from all sin. If we claim we have no sin, we are only fooling ourselves and not living in the truth. But if we confess our sins to him, he is faithful and just to forgive us our sins and to cleanse us from all wickedness. If we claim we have not sinned, we are calling God a liar and showing that his word has no place in our hearts" (1 John 1:6-10).

Ponderings

1. What is porn doing to you?

2. What is your porn doing to others?

3. How do you feel about your participation in sex trafficking when you view porn?

4. What are your thoughts about the chairman elder of the church I pastored who is now in prison for sexual assault against his three daughters?

5. Where do you find yourself today in pornography?

6. What ends to your porn viewing really concern you?

7. What more do you know about pornography than before you read this chapter?

8. What immediate changes will you begin to make? Right now. Today.

Prayer to Pray

Father,

I have defiled myself and abused other people by supporting an industry that enslaves women and children for my enjoyment.

God forgive me.

Help me understand the untold suffering caused by pornography.

Help me see the suffering I cause every time I view pornography.

Help me see past my sexual lusts and see those being used and abused in pornography.

Every woman has a name. Every woman is someone's sister, daughter, or mother.

Help me see the faceless people in my porn viewing.

Oh, God, forgive me.

Make this sink into my heart.

Change my heart, oh, God.

Make me more like You.

Cleanse me from my wicked ways.

Help me love people more than I love myself.

Let me see the end result of my current habits.

Lead me into the way of everlasting life.

So Be It! Amen.

CHAPTER 10

SORROW

"Any mind that is capable of real sorrow is
capable of good."
Harriet Beecher Stowe

"For the kind of sorrow God wants us to experience
leads us away from sin and results in salvation.
There's no regret for that kind of sorrow. But
worldly sorrow, which lacks repentance, results in
spiritual death."
2 Corinthians 7:10

Most men struggling with porn dwell only in the second "sorrow" of 2 Corinthians 7:10; **worldly sorrow**. This is the only sorrow this world offers. This sorrow, however, produces death. This sorrow is marked by guilt, self-loathing, self-hate, sadness, withdrawal, isolation, unhappiness, and death. Every man who has ever spoken with me about his pornography suffers this guilt. As one guy in his mid-30s put it, "I always feel like such a big piece of crap after I spend a few hours in porn." God's Sorrow, however, is grounded in love, correction, discipline, and integrity.

Men feel bad about their pornographic actions. They bear huge amounts of remorse and regret. You feel guilty because you are guilty. When men get caught, sorrow exponentially increases as the consequences for actions appear. Just feeling bad isn't enough, however. God doesn't delight in your living in guilt, remorse, self-loathing, and defeat.

Worldly sorrow is not God's intention. This sorrow leads to just feeling bad—period. It's a horrible place to live. Men living here are often miserable beings. It's a destructive sorrow. "A sorrow of this world" or "worldly sorrow" is a self-condemning, self-defacing, self-accusing, self-defeating, and self-returning sorrow. Since its focus is on self, it always returns to self. Self alone fails to overcome porn. In worldly sorrow, I see men who absolutely hate themselves. In hating yourself, you can't win. Not here. Not at this point. You must move to another place, a better place. Yes, a good sorrow exists! It's there for your grasping and healing. Healing-Sorrow is God's intention for your deliverance and restoration.

Sorrow That Drives Us to God

This sorrow is referred to as "godly sorrow." It is sorrow that drives us to God.[134] Not away from God. Notice its highest attribute. **It leaves no regret**. Wow! It leaves no regret. Really? When is the last time you lived without regret? Now please let this sink in a bit. Imagine sorrow that doesn't allow a residual of shame. No remorse. When is the last time you've felt no regret about your sin?

Godly Sorrow ultimately exists above regret! This is the key element to overcoming any sin problem in your life! Here is your key to overcoming destructive sin. This is, without exception, the missing link in most every man seeking my help or who has spoken with me about his bondage to porn. Or about any sin for that matter.

Godly sorrow is the only way to see yourself, your situation, and your sin. See yourself in full view of God as God sees you. See yourself in Christ Jesus amid your sin. Feel pain the way God feels pain about the life you're living; a life that is so far short of the abundant life God promises you. Feel the hurt God feels when you hurt those around you. Experience anguish with God as you view images that grieve His Holy Spirit. See people, the exploited online people, people whom God created in His image, for His glory, and for His pleasure. Touch God's teardrops pouring from His heavenly eyes streaming down His face as He watches you sell yourself so cheaply before the counterfeit gods of this world.[135] Feel the breaking heart of God who witnesses you losing the wonderful gifts He bestows upon you. Feel the incredible unhappiness such living brings.

It grieved God when He observed the people He created, and saw the poor decisions they made while living in this world. The Bible records, "The LORD observed the extent of human wickedness on the earth, and he saw that everything they thought or imagined was consistently and totally evil … It broke his heart" (Genesis 6:5-6b). Do you ever picture God as a **God with a broken heart**? God's heart breaks when we live in bondage. I believe God suffers more as a result of our addictions, sins, and injuries than we do. Note God's emotions for our weaknesses and sorrows in the following verses. "Yet it was our weaknesses he carried; it was our sorrows that weighed him down…" (Isaiah 53:4). "In all their suffering he also suffered, and he personally rescued them. In his love and mercy he redeemed them. He lifted them up and carried them through all the years" (Isaiah 63:9).

God hurts with us when we hurt. He hurts even when our hurt

is self-inflicted. Even when we provoke God, He grieves. Note the words of Psalm 78:40, "Oh, how often they rebelled against him in the wilderness and grieved his heart in that dry wasteland." The phrase "dry wasteland" can describe the condition of someone living in a porn lifestyle or any sinful lifestyle.

While judgment is part of God's plan to rectify the results of sin, so is grace. God's means for washing those from sin is within a relationship with Jesus Christ. Scripture declares, "Just think how much more the blood of Christ will purify our consciences from sinful deeds so that we can worship the living God. For by the power of the eternal Spirit, Christ offered himself to God as a perfect sacrifice for our sins" (Hebrews 9:14). One day, God will wipe away all tears and sorrows.[136] Our dry wastelands will flourish again. Right now, here and today, you can begin marching out of your dry wasteland towards a flourishing, lush, living garden awaiting you. That choice lies before you in Jesus Christ.[137]

An Ancient Illustration

To further understand the difference between worldly and godly sorrow, let's look at some ancient versions of pornography.

Idolatry, as described and prohibited in the Old Testament, was much more than just bowing before carved handmade images. Bowing before an idol was an act of worship. The Bible is filled with examples of idol worship.

Many of those acts of worship to those idols involved practices we refer to today as pornography. Sexual lewdness was at the center of many ancient religious practices. Often when one thinks of an "idol" in the Bible sense, images of carvings, statues, and paintings come to mind. While not all worship of ancient deities involved lewd forms of sexual activity, many excelled in ancient forms of pornography. Among the ancients, worship of the gods with names like Adonis, Artemis, Asherah, Ashtoreth, Baal, Beelzebub, Chemosh, The Dragon, Marduk, Molech, and many others are associated with declines and demises of nation after nation. Most of these worship systems where nothing more than ancient versions of extreme pornography and sexual exploitation.

Ashtoreth was the goddess of fertility among the Canaanites early in human history. Male and female genitals were part of the many images of this religion. Temple prostitution centered worship on pornography. Worshipers paid for pornography and sex as part of their worship. Child prostitution was rampant. Children were sacrificed to many of the early gods. It plagued God's people, Israel, too. Israel constantly went back into these systems of worship. Open temple prostitution to mass orgies; it was all there. These pagan forms of worship encouraged Israel to unleash unbridled sexual lust in their daily living.

Many forms of ancient Assyrian, Babylonian, and Canaanite idol worship are well embedded in pornographic practices of modern society. Those familiar with the six-minute rave orgy scene in the film *Matrix Reloaded* should know it was nothing more than ancient idol worship. Likewise, Internet pornography is really the same as bowing down to Chemosh or Ashtoreth or The Dragon. Ultimately, it's worshiping one's own sexual self. James warns us, "But each one is tempted when he is carried away and enticed by his own lust. Then when lust has conceived, it gives birth to sin; and when sin is accomplished, it brings forth death. Do not be deceived, my beloved brethren ..." (James 1:15).

The Old Testament King Josiah of Judah dealt harshly to root this problem from his crumbling kingdom. "The king also desecrated the pagan shrines east of Jerusalem, to the south of the Mount of Corruption, where King Solomon of Israel had built shrines for Ashtoreth, the detestable goddess of the Sidonians; and for Chemosh, the detestable god of the Moabites; and for Molech, the vile god of the Ammonites" (2 Kings 23:13). Why? Relationships with these false gods emboldened unrestrained sensuality among their worshipers.

Pornography is nothing new. It's nothing more than idol worship. "You must not make for yourself an idol of any kind or an image of anything in the heavens or on the earth or in the sea" (Exodus 20:4). Too tough you say? Idol worship—regardless of how many times you attend church, how many small group sessions you're involved in, or how many resources you're utilizing—is at the root of your porn problem. Porn is just a fruit. The source of your worship is you. Yes, you. You bow down before porn to consume it upon yourself. This is strong, I know. However, godly sorrow requires seeing pornography the way God sees it. Consider this key verse:

> "Put to death, therefore, whatever belongs to your earthly nature: sexual immorality, impurity, lust, evil desires and greed, which is idolatry" (Colossians 3:5 NIV).

Our earthly nature is inclined to sexual impurity and lust. Connected with these two deficits are evil desires and greed. Why greed? When one partakes in pornography, who is the main recipient of that action? This was at the heart of many ancient forms of idol worship. Ashtoreth poles were erected throughout ancient lands for this type of worship. These poles were constructed for worshiping a deity steeped in sexual debauchery. Temple prostitution, sex slavery, was also a method of temple income. Just like today, pornography revolved around money. "The love of money is the root of all evil" (1 Timothy 6:10). Pornography always finds its core in money.

It's this simple. You're involved in a system of worship that existed thousands of years ago. The Lakshmana Temple in Khajuraho, India is just one shocking example of the extreme debauchery of pornography. Built 1,000 years before the birth of Christ, this temple portrays, in its images, extreme sexual activities of every disturbing kind. The modern pornography phenomenon is a continuation of something old rather than an emergence of something new. This stuff you're struggling with is not new. The dragon slew people long ago, and it continues to rain destruction down today. More than just a habit, more than harmless viewing, more than something men just do—it destroys the very soul.

In its basest form, pornography is your Ashtoreth idol. You bow before the deities of sexual lust, as they did in the Mesopotamia Valley, praising and serving the dragon named Dagon. Simply put, the Porn Dragon is the idol you choose to bow down before every time you enter pornography's world.

And, just as you leave porn only to return, back and forth, the Bible records the nation of Israel ran between the Lord God Almighty and the lesser gods of idol worship. Sometimes a good leader came along to lead Israel into a better path, a God-place, only to see the leader pass off the scene as Israel returned to their old habits. Israel went to God when the nation struggled, suffered national calamity and disaster, only to return to their Baal when things got better. Sound familiar? Read about one of the evilest, murderous kings of Judah:

"Manasseh, (a bad king) was twelve years old when he became king, and he reigned in Jerusalem fifty-five years. His mother was Hephzibah. He did what was evil in the LORD's sight, following the detestable practices of the pagan nations that the LORD had driven from the land ahead of the Israelites. He rebuilt the pagan shrines his father, Hezekiah (a good king), had destroyed. He constructed altars for Baal and set up an Asherah pole, just as King Ahab of Israel had done. He also bowed before all the powers of the heavens and worshiped them" (2 Kings 21:1).

Manasseh gave the people what they wanted. This ensured his tenure as king and guaranteed his fortune and future. Try to picture this king leading the entire nation into worship filled with gross pornography as one of its most common features. Picture a king, a leader, father, and whole families bowing down and worshiping Baal and Ashtoreth.

I chose to use the word "worship" here because modern day pornographic bondage bears so many similarities to idol worship thousands of years ago. Men today often retreat back into God's arms only to leave later. They are doing the same thing the Old Testament people of Israel did. Like a ping-pong ball bouncing back and forth between two paddles on opposite sides of the table, the people ran back and forth between God and those other gods. And today, on one side of the table you seek grace, forgiveness, cleansing, and deliverance, but on the other side you bow down before Ashtoreth, seeking an exhilarating pornographic thrill ride that deadens you a little bit more after each visit.

Is it right, do you think, to use the word "worship" here rather than modern words like addiction, which often portray you as a victim in a helpless state?[138] "Worship" seems more appropriate. Worship carries the idea of serving that which one loves—paying respect, dues, and homage necessary to serve and acquire benefit from it. One of the later kings in Israel's divided history, Josiah of Judah, went on a crusade to rid his land of such practices:

> "The king proceeded to make a clean sweep of all the sex-and-religion shrines that had proliferated east of Jerusalem on the south slope of Abomination Hill, the ones Solomon king of Israel had built to the obscene Sidonian sex goddess Ashtoreth, to Chemosh the dirty-old-god of the Moabites, and to Milcom the depraved god of the Ammonites. He tore apart the altars, chopped down the phallic Asherah-poles, and scattered old bones over the sites. Next, he took care of the altar at the shrine in Bethel that Jeroboam son of Nebat had built—the same Jeroboam who had led Israel into a life of sin. He tore apart the altar, burned down the shrine leaving it in ashes, and then lit fire to the phallic Asherah-pole" (2 Kings 23:12-15 MSG).

The Israelites were no strangers to altars. They understood what happened at an altar. In the Old Testament, an altar was a place where animal, fruit, grain, wine, and other sacrifices were offered to God. There are numerous examples in the Old Testament:

Noah's Altar - Gen. 8:21-22

Abraham's Altar - Gen. 12:6-8; 13:17-18

Isaac's Altar -Gen. 26:23-25

Jacob's Altar - Gen. 28

Moses's Altar - Ex. 20:23-26; 33:7-11

David's Altar - 2 Sam. 24:18-25; Ps. 55:17

Daniel's Altar - Daniel. 6

Elijah's Altar - 1 Kings 17:1

When the people of Israel worshiped on these altars, family life was sound, crime appeared low, society functioned better, and the nation prospered. When Israel strayed into idol worship, based on and steeped in pornographic lifestyles and practices, the nation suffered immeasurably. Sound similar when looking at our world today?

In the New Testament, altars are more metaphorical or a matter of imagery. It is simply a place, time, or method to meet God personally. An altar is a decision to worship.

So, we must ask the question. At which altar are you worshiping? Before you exists two clear altars. Two clearly diametrically opposed ways of worshiping.

One altar is centered upon self.

The other altar is centered upon the One True God.

One altar promotes unabated sensuality without restriction.

The other altar promotes relationship, marriage, and family.

Leave your altar of self, "So let us come boldly to the throne of our gracious God. There we will receive his mercy, and we will **find grace to help** us when we need it most" (Hebrews 4:16). Everyone should memorize this verse. Let it become a mainstay for those struggling with a habitual sin. It is God's Altar of Grace for us today. It is an altar where we can find help every single time we need it. An Altar of Grace that helps when we can't help ourselves.

And before we leave this section, consider the high cost of not making the right choice. Pornography always carries a price attached. How many times have you paid for sex? "Oh, not me," you say. "All my viewing is free!" On the contrary, worshiping these types of idols always carries a high price. Figure in the cost of your computer, the Internet, your time, subscriptions, and clearly, you will find pornography costs. Figure in the human cost of those forced into "the industry" to make pornographic viewing possible. The costs devastates its victims. And think of the future costs: the personal, relational costs of marriage, family, relationship, and integrity figure heavily into liabilities.

Godly Sorrow

Bluntly put, the source of your Porn Dragon is you, my friend. It has its very existence, strength, and being in you. You feed it, care for it, play with it, and spend time with it. Jesus taught this very truth. Notice His words, "And then He added, 'It is what comes from inside that defiles you. For from within, out of a person's heart, come evil thoughts, sexual immorality, theft, murder, adultery, greed, wickedness, deceit, lustful desires, envy, slander, pride, and foolishness. All these vile things come from within; they are what defile you'" (Mark 7:21-24). Just as the ancient idols were worshiped, so, too, your habit is a form of worship. Think about it. See it the way God does. And, again, see the direction it takes you.

The Bible records, "Manasseh also sacrificed his own sons in the fire in the valley of Ben-Hinnom" (2 Chronicles 33:6). He sacrificed his sons in the valley Jesus referred to as a place "where the fire never dies, and worms are not quenched" (Mark 9:44). Sacrificing of children made up a large part of these types of religious practices in the ancient days as did so many other ancient idol-centered religions. Young children were slaughtered before the gods and goddesses of Ashtoreth and Baal. The slaughter continues to this day before a modern-day Porn Dragon. Women and children are the victims fueling the current worldwide porn phenomenon. It's tragically interesting that children were also the victims of pornographic bondage from the earliest years of human civilization.

Is this language too strong? Some men tell me this. "Wow! You make me feel like a crud!"

My answer is, "No, I see who you are in Jesus, and what you can become in Christ, if you make Him Lord of your whole life." Your porn practices condemn you and your heart. Your porn life destroys everything you claim to love. One church leader, arrested for sexual assault upon a minor, cried, "I just can't control my forbidden compulsions." Let it sink in deeply. When the weight of porn's virtual inevitability presses heavily upon you, godly sorrow is near. King David, after confessing his sexual sins, understood this. He wrote, "The sacrifice you desire is a broken spirit. You will not reject a broken and repentant heart, O God" (Psalm 51:17). Godly Sorrow is a crushing and breaking of the spirit causing total dependence upon God. Are you there yet? It's time to act upon it. Don't wait until it's too late.

Good News!

Are you feeling cruddy about all of this? God is greater than how you feel right now. Our God is greater than those other gods. He's able to mend and repair you. He's able to put you back together again. He can redeem you. He can restore. And, what's even better, God is willing, waiting, and wanting to do more than you can possibly think. This promise is given to us in Scripture:

> "If our hearts condemn us, we know that God is greater than our hearts, and he knows everything … if our hearts do not condemn us, we have confidence before God and receive from him anything we ask, because we keep his commands and do what pleases him" (1 John 3:20-22).

It is only our sin that condemns us. God's intent is for us to live beyond condemnation.[139] When God is our center, accusatory condemnation is not present. Our relationship with Him is rich and rewarding. When we find our delight in Him; He satisfies our lives. "Commit your way to the LORD, Trust also in Him, and He will do it" (Psalms 37:4).

Key Essentials

Sorrow and guilt can drive you toward godly repentance. Throw yourself upon God's loving grace. Seek forgiveness in full confession of your pornographic activities. Sense God's love for you. See Jesus Christ putting his arm around you, looking at your sin, He says, "Wow! That's a lot of sin! We need to work on that together. You see, I paid for all your sins on the cross. Really; your sins are gone. You are free from it. Now, we just have to get you to realize the freely loved and valued person that you are. We will take these next steps together. Let's begin because, 'There is no condemnation for those who belong to Christ Jesus. And because you belong to him, the power of the life-giving Spirit has freed you from the power of sin that leads to death'" (Romans 1:1-2).

Scripture for Reflection

"For his anger lasts only a moment, but his favor lasts a lifetime! Weeping may last through the night, but joy comes with the morning" (Psalm 30:5).

Ponderings

1. Describe some of some your possible altars.

2. Which altar do you worship on?

3. How does this interfere with the worship of God?

4. What does worldly sorrow feel like to you?

5. How does worldly sorrow defeat you?

6. How does this type of sorrow condemn you?

7. What might life be like if there were no condemnation in your life?

8. Do you feel that God loves you enough to forgive you and help you?

Prayer to Pray

Oh, God,

I now understand that my pornography is just another form of idol worship. I am guilty of worshiping some of the same false idols that people bowed before 4,000 years ago. I didn't understand this God until now.

My sorrow has slayed me over and over again.

Worldly sorrow leaves me dead inside.

Help me to see my sin the way you see it in my life.

Give me your sorrow over my sin.

Help me repent and turn from this stuff.

In your sorrow, there is no regret. I want to live without regret.

So be it! – Amen."

CHAPTER 11

THE ESSENTIAL INGREDIENT: PRAYER

"Anything is a blessing which makes us pray."
C. H. Spurgeon

"And even when you ask, you don't get it because
your motives are all wrong – you want only what
will give you pleasure."
James 4:3

"You can pray for anything, and if you have faith,
you will receive it."
Matthew 21:22

"Don't worry about anything; instead, pray about
everything. Tell God what you need, and thank him
for all he has done.
Then you will experience God's peace, which exceeds
anything we can understand. His peace will guard
your hearts and minds as you live in Christ Jesus."
Philippians 4:6-7

In this chapter is your blueprint for effective prayer. This simple, step-by-step method for practical, purposeful, and simple life-changing prayer will empower you to succeed. The key is replacing your time spent in pornography with time in prayer to God.

When I mention the "P" word, men often exhibit frustration. During a session with about 20 men, I heard a fellow let out a groan, moaning, "You mean you're going to tell us all we have to do is PRAY! SORRY! Heard that before! It doesn't work! Just saying!"

Smiling, I gently asked, "How goes your prayer life?"

Looking down, he replied, "Not very good."

Most men think of prayer as a formal set time each day spent on your knees praying through an interminable list. Prayer like that seems, at first, impractical, improbable, and impossible. Yet, please listen to the words of Jesus, who says, "But if you remain in me and my words remain in you, you may ask for anything you want, and it will be granted" (John 15:7)!

See Jesus' words, "You may ask for anything you want ..." The word "want" is translated from the Greek word *thelo* and means a wish, will, or desire. In some versions of the Bible, it is translated with those words.[140]

Anything you desire ... what do you desire? Here is the caveat. Jesus' one stipulation is that you remain (the Greek word here is *meno*) in him. In other words, your relationship with Jesus Christ is so mega-dependent upon him, that you literally can ask anything! Jesus' use of the word "remain" is crucial here for proper understanding and application.

The word *meno* is used well over 100 times in the New Testament. It is translated in a variety of ways to help express the meaning of the context in which the word appears. Here are several English translations used in the Bible:

1. Abide
2. Dwell
3. Continue
4. Endure
5. Continue
6. Stay
7. Wait
8. Rest

Jesus' idea when He said, "If you remain …" is living and staying with Him. Continuing with Christ on your life journey is Jesus' meaning. To this day, I have yet to meet one person struggling with an addiction who could say, "I am resting in Jesus Christ. I am focused on Him."

This is usually what happens. A guy wades or jumps into porn's cesspool. Inevitable guilt, shame, and blame will follow. Then he tries some desperate emergency prayers for help. He makes a resolve to quit, and for a time feels better attending church, prayer group, small group, or recovery group. Days or weeks later, the porn activity resumes. This cycle is repeated many times. Finally, he reaches a false conclusion: "Prayer does not work."

My response is, "That's not prayer. That's you talking to yourself, asking to feel better about yourself."

Remaining Prayer

The prayer Jesus spoke of in John 15:7 is prayer anchored in continuance. Continuance in an active, lively, relationship with Jesus Christ breathes life into prayer. Your relationship with Christ is everything. Remaining Prayer is so focused on the person of Jesus

Christ that His words continue with us. "And my words remain in you," is the inevitable result of remaining in Jesus Christ. If you desire Christ, and continue in His words (listen to this), you can ASK ANYTHING!

The first promise, "Ask anything." Bring your porn to God! God is bigger than porn! God can handle it! He knows more about porn and its destructive end for humanity, than you do. And the bottom line is, your problem really isn't porn. Yes, I did say that. Your problem is not a porn problem. Your problem is a lack of depth in Jesus Christ problem.

Simple Remaining Prayer will change your thinking and attitude towards pornography. It will redirect your thoughts towards Jesus each time you find yourself tempted to consider porn's cesspool. Through Remaining Prayer, absolute dependence upon Christ, a way of escaping pornography will appear. Finding a way out of pornography is a clear Bible plan of dealing with sin. "The temptations in your life are no different from what others experience. And God is faithful. He will not allow the temptation to be more than you can stand. When you are tempted, He will show you a way out so that you can endure" (1 Corinthians 10:13).

It means every time you're tempted to tap your smartphone to enter porn's dungeon once again; you will replace that urge with Remaining Prayer. The Bible tells us to "pray without ceasing" (1 Thessalonians 5:17). Jesus taught that prayer is the means for overcoming discouragement: "One day Jesus told his disciples a story to show that they should always pray and never give up" (Luke 18:1).

Now, perhaps you're thinking, "There's no way I'm turning myself into a monk!" That's one of the huge problems with inaccurate ideas about prayer. Remaining Prayer is much more practical than lofty words read on Sunday morning at church. Think of Jesus while suffering and dying on the cross. He simply prayed, "Father, forgive these people. They don't know what they are doing." Jesus' recorded prayers are usually short and to the point. Most prayers recorded in the Bible are, in fact, short and to the point. Also, many prayers are simple pleas for help and understanding. Let's look at a clear and simple plan for prayer found in Philippians.

Prayer Replaces Worry

Pray when you worry, are anxious, or tempted. Immediately begin asking God for help—every single time: "Don't worry (or be anxious) about anything; instead, pray about everything" (Philippians 4:6).

See the conflict? It's bound in the words "anything" and "everything." Most men, struggling with pornography, live in constant anxiety. The simple command here is to "knock it off." Just stop your worry, stop the anxiety, and stop the guilt.

The formula for accomplishing this is quite simple. Every single time you find yourself worried, anxious or tempted, bring this to God immediately. Talk with God about what's in your heart. Speak verbally aloud if alone. If you are in a public place, talk to God within yourself. In this way, you can pray many times a day. A simple prayer like, "God, I am worried again about _____, so I am talking with you about it" can be as effective as a long, wordy address. Or, say something like, "Jesus, I want porn again so …" and ask for strength to resist. Note the formula for this type of praying in Philippians 5:6-7: "Be anxious for nothing, but in everything by prayer and supplication, with thanksgiving, let your requests be made known to God; and the peace of God, which surpasses all understanding, will guard your hearts and minds through Christ Jesus (NKJV)."

Tell God What You Need!

It's that simple. **Just tell God what you need at the time you need it.** Every time you find yourself tempted, tell God, "God I am really worried about …" or, "God, I want to look at porn again. I mean, I really want it. This is not good for my family or me, and it brings sorrow to You. Give me your heart here, God, help me."

As a person struggling with anger daily, James learned to pray effectively every time he felt angry. He told me, "I wake up angry every day. Every time I find myself beginning to burn with irritation deep down inside, I pray. I say, 'God the enemy (anger) is back. Quiet it down, please. Calm me inside right now.'"

Sometimes he prayed aloud. Most times he prayed within himself. He prayed dozens of times every day until he gained victory and control over his anger. He learned connected, consistent, Remaining Prayer.

Another man shared, "I guess the reason I like porn so much is because I wish a woman like that loved me." This revealed a deficit in his life. His prayer went something like, "God I am lonely again, and want to be loved. I need to be loved. I want someone to be interested in me. I feel empty and want to return to my porn. Porn is not real. Your love and plan for my life is real. Help me to see that I am loved by you. Porn isn't real. You are real."

Thank God For What He's Done

Gratitude is the second essential to effective praying. The Bible encourages an attitude of thankfulness in all situations: "In everything give thanks: for this is the will of God in Christ Jesus concerning you" (1 Thessalonians 5:18 KJV).

Notice "everything" is mentioned again. While praying about everything and thanking in everything, we learn gratitude. Thank

God for your struggles. Struggling forces you to look for help beyond yourself. Thank God for your losses, too. In loss, one appreciates possession. Thank Him for the events driving you to turn away from your destructive habits. Thank Him for forgiveness, both God's and others. Thank Him for your struggle. The struggle helps you see your problem. It's helping you deal with it. Thank Him for the gift of sexuality and the ability to love someone else. Give thanks for every good thing around you. See the good stuff in your world. Thank God for forgiveness. Thank Him for His love, for His compassion, and for His mercy. Thank God for the second, third, and umpteenth start overs. Gratitude is the secret.

This is a huge struggle for many of us living in first world cultures, especially in the United States. Our consumer society conditions us to believe that my needs, wants, and desires supersede every other consideration around me. What I want is primary in my life, and everyone else's for that matter. I can only be thankful for the things I like. My life focuses only on me and on the stuff I want. Living in this dimension demotes gratitude. Gratitude becomes elusive and self-focused.

As you tell God your needs, learn to find gratitude in that same need. Yes, be thankful for your struggle with pornography. That is correct. Express gratitude for the struggle, "Thank You, God, for my struggle with pornography because to struggle shows me my need for You." Struggle brings you to a place of needing God. The struggle brings you to a place of needing people. In struggle, as you gain victory, you can help many others slain by the same lifestyle. "In everything give thanks…" not just the good stuff, but the bad stuff, too. In the bad stuff of life, we can learn the value of the good stuff of life. In learning to value the good stuff of life, we learn to appreciate and enjoy living. Now, ask yourself, "When was the last time I really gave thanks for anything?"

In Christ, you possess everything you need to overcome! Remaining Prayer is the means of accessing Christ's power in your life. It's a matter of your focus and praying, if you're praying at all. Most people who are struggling pray very little. Prayer which fails to put Christ at the center of your life is powerless prayer. Christ at your center is the essence of Remaining Prayer.

This is Lordship; making Christ Lord of your life. Jesus living at the center of your life is the key to answered prayers. When you learn to pray consistently and effectively, Jesus takes his rightful place in your life. Jesus becomes Lord in your life. He takes his rightful place over your life. Consider who or what is lord of your life. What preoccupies your thoughts? What takes most your time and energy?

When I was pastoring in northern Minnesota, a man in my congregation continually talked about fishing and hunting. This guy ate and slept hunting and fishing. Most every weekend, you'd find him on the lake in his expensive bass boat. During hunting season, he was always gone hunting. His obituary read, "He lived for hunting and fishing." Most who knew him agreed. Fishing and hunting occupied his total person.

For those in bondage to pornography, the answer is painfully simple. "Pornography is lord of your life. Porn is the god you bow before and worship." Are you focusing only on making money, then money is your lord? If that job and getting ahead is all you think about, then career is your lord. Is social media gaining all your time? Maybe those "friends" on Facebook have become the lord of your life. What preoccupies you? Where do you spend most of your time? Remaining Prayer requires Jesus at the center of your life.

Key Essentials

Scripture commands us to, "to put off your old self, which belongs to your former manner of life and is corrupt through deceitful desires" (Ephesians 4:22 ESV). Closing avenues of porn's access in your life is part of the "putting off" process. However, when putting off things, a vacuum is created. Unless the emptiness created by removing porn is filled, failure often follows. When putting off bad practices, you must put on something else in its place. The Bible teaches, "Put on the new self, created after the likeness of God in true righteousness and holiness" (Ephesians 4:24 ESV). The process for renewing is sandwiched in between these two verses where the text says, "And to be renewed in the spirit of your minds" (Ephesians 4:23 ESV).

Renewal is the goal. Remaining Prayer—continual dependence upon Christ—renews. Eliminating pornography exposure and replacing it with simple conversational prayer will focus your heart on God. Remaining Prayer dwells in Christ. If you're not abiding and remaining in Christ at this moment, where are you? Everyone dwells somewhere.

Scripture for Reflection

"But if you remain in me and my words remain in you, you may ask for anything you want, and it will be granted!" (John 15:7).

Ponderings

1. How can you develop Remaining Prayer in your life?

2. How can you pray about everything?

3. What do you worry about?

4. What causes you anxiety?

5. How can you replace anxiety with prayer?

6. What are your needs?

7. How can you tell God what you need?

8. What can you thank God for in your life?

9. Take inventory of all the good things in your life.

10. How can you put off porn?

11. How can you put on a new nature created to be like God?

12. Where do you remain today?

Prayer to Pray

God,

Here I am again staring porn straight in the eyes. I want it, but I know it's not good for me.

God, I need your help or I will succumb to this evil thing once again.

Help me turn now from my dragon.

Help me put off my old self.

Help me to become the new person you intend me to be.

Help me put on that new person.

Penetrate my thoughts with your thoughts.

Help me become a Jesus dweller, not a porn dweller.

I choose right now, to remain in Jesus. I choose your Son's words over the words of this world.

So be it – Amen."

CHAPTER 12

RENEWAL

"And so, dear brothers and sisters, I plead with you
to give your bodies to God because of all he has
done for you. Let them be a living and holy sacrifice-
-the kind he will find acceptable. This is truly the
way to worship him. Don't copy the behavior and
customs of this world, but let God transform you
into a new person by changing the way you think.
Then you will learn to know God's will for you,
which is good and pleasing and perfect."
Romans 12:1-2

Men often ask, "How can I pray about all this stuff?" One helpful encouragement is found in the above phrase, "Because of all He has done for you." Remaining Prayer at its core focuses on God. Focusing on God is where power lies to conquer your dragon. Effective prayer changes the way you think.

Transforming your old way of thinking, that was slaying you, requires a spiritual process. As one young man improved in his struggles against pornography, he called Remaining Prayer his "Prayer Therapy." This Prayer Therapy involved several steps. Wherever and whenever he found himself struggling with impure thoughts, he trained himself to:

1. Immediately thank God for His goodness.
2. Ask for God's help and grace with his thought life.
3. Ask God's forgiveness for straying again into the world's cesspool of sin.
4. Finished by thanking God for his unconditional love.

This continuous practice molded him into a Christian man whose sexuality was placed under the Lordship of Jesus Christ. Today, he enjoys a wonderful marriage, family, and ministry helping other men escape pornography's clutches.

BACKS helps develop the spiritual processes in your thinking. As you reduce porn in your life, repetitive Remaining Prayer replaces the idols, that once filled your life, with Jesus Christ. Remaining Prayer is the conduit by which all victories are possible.

New thinking focused upon Scripture changes your heart and mind towards your Porn Dragon. After some time, your desire to access porn will diminish. Your desire to dwell in porn changes into a desire to dwell in Christ. **Many men testify that the process reduces their impulses towards pornography. In fact, many men share that after one year of spiritual renewal, their lustful tendencies seem to "just disappear from the mind."**

Some recent discoveries in Neuroplasticity in the last few decades seem to agree with the renewing principle of Romans 12:1-2. Neuroplasticity is "the brain's ability to reorganize itself by forming new neural connections throughout life."[141]

Neuroplasticity points to a "renewed mind." It's the brain's ability to restructure itself with repetitive training and practice. It's one of the most popular areas of psychology today. Written almost two thousand years ago, Paul possessed some insight into the brains' malleable qualities. Simply put, with training, practice, and God's help, your brain can change how it thinks. Changing how you think, changes how you behave.

Prayer, dependence upon God, and repetitious renewing of the mind, eliminates dependence upon porn. Eliminating porn replaces this idol with true God worship. There is hope. Prayer's fulcrum is Romans 12:1-2.

The Goal—Giving your body back to God

Paul begs believers to give their bodies back to God. The foundation for giving here is gratitude. The request is reasonable because according to Scripture your body doesn't belong to you anyway:

"Don't you realize that your bodies are actually parts of Christ? Should a man take his body, which is part of Christ, and join it to a prostitute? Never! And don't you realize that if a man joins himself to a prostitute, he becomes one body with her? For the Scriptures say, "The two are united into one." But the person who is joined to the Lord is one spirit with him. Run from sexual sin! No other sin so clearly affects the body as this one does. For sexual immorality is a sin against your own body. Don't you realize that your body is the temple of the Holy Spirit, who lives in you and was given to you by God? You do not belong to yourself, for God bought you with a high price. So you must honor God with your body" (1 Corinthians 6:15-20).

Contrary to popular thinking, as a Christian, your body does not belong to you. It belongs to God. Do you disagree with that last statement? Tell me, who gave you your athletic ability? Yes, you worked at developing skills. Yet, for some reason, health, stamina, and ability are yours. Where did that come from? Why was another born to spend life in a wheelchair while you were born with athletic superiority?

Your beauty—where did that originate? The individual who sings beautifully and becomes a pop sensation can hardly claim his or her talent is self-created. You either can sing, or you can't, period. Everyone can make some melodic noise, but superstar talents owe gratitude to another—their Creator. Our sexuality is a gift from God, too. It does not belong to us.

This is a core concept of Bible teaching. When one puts their faith in Jesus Christ, new life occurs. Jesus Christ paid the high purchase price. His willingness to die for you justifies God's ownership. Upon faith in Christ, the Holy Spirit enters into God's temple, your body. It's within your body that God's Holy Spirit lives. This new life in Christ was brutally expensive to purchase on our behalf. Through the loss of dignity, separation from His Father, brutal suffering, and a horrible death, Jesus bought our freedom from sin. Paul taught, "Now you are free from your slavery to sin, and you have become slaves to righteous living" (Romans 6:18). For this reason, Paul begs Christians to give their bodies back to God.

Learn Gratitude

Gratitude is foundational to prayer. In the American culture, gratitude is rare. We are taught as consumers to demand, complain, and fuss when things are not to our liking. In our political arena, continual, caustic, verbal sparring between the two major parties encourages an attitude of entitlement. American media suspects everything, questions everything, and looks for the most salacious stories of betrayal, victimization, and wrongdoing. When is the last time you heard a president, senator, congressman, news anchor, or any other person for that matter, show gratitude for their respective positions in life?

When did you last take inventory of all God has done for you? Try making a list of God's goodness in your life. Take your journal, piece of paper, your iPad, or your smartphone and begin listing everything good that comes to your mind. Get a hold of Paul's words, *"I plead with you to give your bodies to God because of all he has done for you."* What has God done for you?

> Look at your church, "Thank you, God!"
> Look at your marriage, "Thank you, Lord!"
> Look at your children, "Thank you, God!"
> How about your health? "Thank you, God!"
> What about your job? "Thank you, God!"
> How about just the ability to eat breakfast this morning?

1. If you had breakfast today, you possess something a billion people do not—adequate food and water.

2. If you sat with family, you possess a blessing hundreds of thousands suffering in the Middle East conflict do not—family.

3. If you partook of your breakfast with your own faculties, you performed a function many cannot—you fed yourself.

4. If you left the breakfast table satisfied, congratulations. You experienced a sensation another billion people never experience. You possess more than you actually need.

5. If you left your home with money in your pocket, congratulations, you are in the top 10 percent income level in the world.

What else comes to your mind? Did someone express an action of love towards you? "Thank you, God!"

Examine your closest friendships, "Oh, God, YOU are good!" Look at your standing before God in Jesus Christ, "All praise to God, the Father of our Lord Jesus Christ, who has blessed us with every spiritual blessing in the heavenly realms because we are united with Christ" (Ephesians 1:3). A gracious attitude turns focus from one's self towards another. Consider these verses as your guide to gracious thanksgiving:

> "Be thankful in all circumstances, for this is God's will for you who belong to Christ Jesus" (1 Thessalonians 5:18).

> "Don't worry about anything; instead, pray about everything. Tell God what you need, and thank him for all he has done" (Philippians 4:6).

> "And give thanks for everything to God the Father in the name of our Lord Jesus Christ" (Ephesians 5:20).

A gracious mind, continually discovering reasons for thankfulness, fills a mind's compulsion, causing it to wander into healthy areas. Replace porn's lust with a continual inventory of God's goodness. Be thankful! There exist plenty of reasons for gratitude if you take the time to look.

Redirect Your Worship

The word "worship" comes from an old English word meaning "worthship" or "worthiness."[142] What you value as worthy defines your worship. You look at pornography because you value it. This culture teaches that pornography is a natural and safe practice for men. Romans 12:1-2 contradicts this. Porn is a false form of worship focused upon your own lust.

The Bible is quite clear that only One Being is worthy of our worship. The Old Testament prophet Isaiah witnessed angels in the Temple worshiping God as they cried out, "Holy, holy, holy is the LORD of Heaven's Armies! The whole earth is filled with his glory!" (Isaiah 6:3). As he worshiped and experienced God, it revealed his own shortcomings. Notice Isaiah's reaction, "Then I said, "It's all over! I am doomed, for I am a sinful man. I have filthy lips, and I live among a people with filthy lips. Yet I have seen the King, the Lord of Heaven's Armies" (Isaiah 6:5). True worship brings renewal and change.

As you redirect your worship from yourself, removing idols of this culture from your presence, your Porn Dragon diminishes in strength, scope, and power. It's at that point you begin learning God's good and perfect will for your life. This good and perfect will is free from the counterfeit pleasures pornography offers along with its temporary, empty, and destructive pleasures.

Changing one's object of worship is challenging. Think about it this way. How many long hours, nights, days, months, and years did you spend acquiring your pursuit of pornography? What skills did you acquire to access more porn? What skills did you master to hide your porn? What lies did you learn to tell yourself and significant others to deny or justify your porn?

Do you see your dedication here? Your worship required dedication. Didn't it? In dedication to the Porn Dragon, you ended up exactly where you are right now.

Redirecting your worship back to God requires at least this level of dedication. The good news is that you can do it. There are several amazing actions working for you.

There is added strength: "**I can do everything through Christ, who gives me strength**" (Philippians 4:13). If you put your faith in Christ, a Victor lives within you, one who already conquered this foe. "You have already won a victory over those people, because the Spirit who lives in you is greater than the spirit who lives in the world" (1 John 4:4 ESV). Take that to the bank, my friend! God's Spirit living in your life is greater than all this unseemly stuff. You must learn to access this power.

Identify Counterfeits

"Don't copy the ways of this world." James talks about this, "So don't be misled, my dear brothers and sisters. Whatever is good and perfect is a gift coming down to us from God our Father, who created all the lights in the heavens. He never changes or casts a shifting shadow" (James 1:16-17). God's gifts do not cast a shifting shadow.

Everything porn offers you counterfeits God's intended goodness for your life. That's why porn casts such a huge shifting shadow over your life right now. What are the counterfeits porn offers? Sexual pleasure? How do you feel after viewing porn and masturbating? If you're like most men who speak with me, you feel pretty lousy. Why? Porn offers companionship, but at what cost? Cyber-companionship is an illusion filled with guilt and self-abasement.

Counterfeiting is Satan's specialty. The Apostle Paul warns, "Even

Satan disguises himself as an angel of light" (2 Corinthians 11:13-14). Paul also calls Satan, "The god of this age" (2 Corinthians 4:4). So many vices, abuses, and addictions point towards the god of this world's success and implementation of counterfeit plans for our lives.

Surrender Yourself Repeatedly to God

In the middle of Romans 12:2 Paul encourages, "let God transform you ..." This speaks of surrender. Surrendering yourself to God is necessary for transformation. There is no middle ground. You serve who or what you surrender yourself to.

God rarely kicks down the door of your life, forcing Himself into a place of respect. The prophet Jonah in the Old Testament is one of many examples of how God works to get our attention. God graciously worked with Jonah to bring him to the only hope Israel had against their brutal adversary, the Assyrians.

The capital of Assyria at that time was Nineveh. A megacity by ancient standards, God called Jonah to go to the city of his adversaries and to share God's forgiving love. The brutality of the Assyrian Empire was much on par with the events occurring in the Middle East at the hands of ISIS today. King Jeroboam II ruled Israel, and the kingdom was in decline on all fronts. Israel simply did not possess the means to stand against Assyria. Repeatedly, Assyria attacked Israel leaving devastation and sorrow behind. God expressed a plan to Jonah, "Go to Nineveh! Tell them to repent, turn from this stuff, or I will destroy them!" Jonah, failing to see God's good intention to protect Israel, refused. Imagine! Either your enemies turn from their ways, or they will perish! This action, on the part of Jonah, sounds like a great solution. Right? Yet, even with clear direction from God, Jonah refused. God used several extreme interactions, including a whale, to bring Jonah to a better place. God is willing to do this for you as well.

Ponderings

Think about this for a moment:

1. How many times did you willfully surrender yourself to your dragon's desires?

2. How many times did you fall before him in total captivity and willingness?

Leave the dragon and give God that dedication and surrender! If you commit your heart to God, He will begin to change the person you are into the person He desires you to become.

3. Are you willing to let God transform you into a new person by changing the way you think?

This is when you will begin to learn God's good intentions for you and your life. See your loving Father in the mix. You are not alone. Grab hold of this Bible verse. Learn it. Repeat it. Take heart. Take hope.

> "For I know the plans I have for you," says the LORD. "They are plans for good and not for disaster, to give you a future and a hope" (Jeremiah 29:11).

CHAPTER 13

THE BOTTOM LINE

"And now, dear brothers and sisters, one final thing.
Fix your thoughts on what is true, and honorable,
and right, and pure, and lovely, and admirable.
Think about things that are excellent and worthy
of praise. Keep putting into practice all you learned
and received from me—everything you heard from
me and saw me doing. Then the God of peace will
be with you."
Philippians 4:8-9

Once, when I was teaching BACKS to a group of men, an older gentleman approached me after the fourth session. Like a sales agent, he barked out, "So, what's the bottom line here?" Looking for a quick fix, he wanted a simple and immediate remedy to evict his dragon from his heart's premises. Philippians 4:8-9 is that bottom line. For most Christians, this "one final thing" seems a difficult path to ascend. Yet, I maintain the bottom line here is not that difficult. Look carefully.

Practice **daily renewal**. Paul, in his letter to people in the church at Philippi, concludes, "Keep putting into practice …" Here's the winning element. Practice brings proficiency. The Greek word for "practice" is *prasso*, or "exercise." It means to be busy with or occupied by doing something. Just as you may go to the fitness club or local YMCA, you must develop a routine of spiritual practice. Practicing bad habits brought you where you are today. Practicing good and godly habits, through prayerful dependence upon God, will bring you to a better, more satisfying place. Remaining Prayer will go a long way toward helping you, "keep putting into practice" the five-step BACKS approach in this book.

Fix Your Thoughts

The word "fix" is also translated, in other versions of the Bible, to "dwell" or "meditate." We have seen that dwelling word before. Where is your mental/spiritual dwelling? To dwell means to make one's dwelling or abode in a particular place. Begin to make your dwelling in better places than in past days. Remaining Prayer seeks to direct your dwelling place in Jesus Christ. By fixing your thoughts on what is true, and honorable, and right, and pure, and lovely, and admirable, and thinking about things that are excellent and worthy of praise; this new spiritual and mental abode can be yours.

What is true? Pornography does not offer a true relationship. It is not satisfying. It does not portray women truthfully. Pornography is populated with unhappy people. Porn is not harmless; it's exploitive. It is not beautiful. It is not happy. It is not relational. Fill your mind and heart only with truth. Ask yourself, "Is that which I am viewing truthful?" Jesus said, "I am the way the truth and the life …" (John 16:6).

What is Honorable? This word means "respectful." Are your viewing habits and actions respectful of God, others, and yourself?

Pornography respects no one. Learn to respect every person created in God's image as God's child.

Is it Right? In every activity begin asking yourself, "Is this right?" You know the answer. Develop the habit of asking yourself this question every time you engage with media. Put your name in the beginning of the question, "_____ , is this right?" Any hesitation other than an immediate "yes" is suspect.

Is this Pure? Pure, free from contaminants, is the idea here. Gold is only valuable if it's pure. While in South Africa, years ago, we visited Gold Reef City Mines in Johannesburg. There we witnessed the process of melting down gold to remove all the impurities and contaminants from the raw ore. Intense heat ensures purity. Only after a rigorous process does gold become highly valuable. Purify your life.

Is this lovely? Again, in South Africa, among the English-speaking community, there exists a common word for approval. It is the word "lovely." When something was acceptable or pleasing, a person often responded, "That's lovely." Remaining Prayer seeks lovely thoughts, actions, and results.

Is this Admirable? Can you speak well of your activity? Is what you're involved in something producing pride or guilt?

Think About. This indicates a process. While the word "think" here carries several connotations, one of its meanings is "dwell." Here we are again; remaining and dwelling. What are you dwelling on right now? If it doesn't fall into the above categories, pray to Jesus right now, asking for God's help. "God help me think about better things." The level of thought desired by God in our thought life is anchored in two expressions:

1. **Is this excellent?** The word "excellent" has a rich history, especially among ancient people. "The most articulated value in Greek culture is *arête*; the word actually has a meaning closer to 'being the best you can be,' or 'reaching your highest potential.'"[143] God desires you to become the best you can be. He wants you to reach your highest potential, and He gives you the path to accomplish this in Philippians 4:8-9: Think only on those things that bring excellence. God's heart for your life is so much bigger and more beautiful than where you are right now. Be the person God sees you are in Christ Jesus.

2. **Is this praise-worthy?** In our culture, much like the culture of Jesus' day, people seek praise from others. The Greeks were obsessed with praise. Christians should seek God's approval only. This is the meaning of "praise-worthy."[144] Does what your thinking about bring God's praise for you?

CONCLUSION

Ultimately, the dragon will be defeated. The Bible promises this! While the dragon holds incredible power now, the beast's reign upon this world is limited by God. It will ultimately come to an end. He is, in fact, already defeated. His end, coming in and culminating in a great battle in heaven, is assured. The Bible tells of the battle:

"Then there was war in heaven. Michael and his angels fought against the dragon and his angels. And the dragon lost the battle, and he and his angels were forced out of heaven. This great dragon—the ancient serpent called the devil, or Satan, the one deceiving the whole world—was thrown down to the earth with all his angels" (Revelation 12:7-9).

"Then I saw an angel coming down from heaven with the key to the bottomless pit and a heavy chain in his hand. He seized the dragon—that old serpent, who is the devil, Satan—and bound him in chains for a thousand years. The angel threw him into the bottomless pit, which he then shut and locked so Satan could not deceive the nations anymore until the thousand years were finished" (Revelation 20:1-3).

"Then the devil, who had deceived them, was thrown into the fiery lake of burning sulfur, joining the beast and the false prophet. There they will be tormented day and night forever and ever" (Revelation 20:10).

The dragon is clearly on the losing side. His end results in a horrible, well-deserved, tormenting containment forever. Never again will the dragon enjoy freedom to harm and destroy. Never again will another child be harmed. Never again will disease ravage a healthy body. Never again will temptation approach us. Evil will cease. Only goodness will remain. With the dragon gone, so will its ruinous powers cease. He is finished forever! Good news! Great news! Encouraging news!

Here's more good news. Your dragon possesses, this very moment, only the power you extend to it. When you drop your boundaries, the dragon feeds off you. Pulling away from your dragon and learning to resist its presence deprives it of power. "Resist the devil, and he will flee from you" (James 4:7). God's power is available to you. If you choose to leverage God's power through His Son Jesus Christ, victory is yours. The following verses off three great promises of hope that prevail when you are nestled in God's person:

"But you belong to God, my dear children. **You have already won a victory** over those people because the **Spirit who lives in you is greater** than the spirit who lives in the world" (1 John 4:4).

"For every child of God defeats this evil world, and we achieve this victory through our faith" (1 John 5:4).

"We know that God's children do not make a practice of sinning, for God's Son holds them securely, and the evil one cannot touch them" (1 John 5:18).

Promise number one states, "You've already won the victory." Success is yours. You only need to grasp it. **Promise number two**

says, "God's Spirit dwelling within you ensures victory." God's Spirit guarantees success. Paul writes to the Galatians, "So I say, let the Holy Spirit guide your lives. Then you won't be doing what your sinful nature craves" (Galatians 5:16). **The third promise** is victory's immanency. Victory is yours right now, today, this very moment. Notice the words, "He cannot touch you." Think about that for just a moment. Unless you allow it, the dragon cannot touch you. The torments of pornography, or any other addictions, for that matter, hold zero power over you unless you empower the dragon.

What's the bottom line? How is success guaranteed? What does it take to overcome pornography in your life? Triumph depends upon this one pivotal question. Do you belong to Jesus Christ? Belonging is everything. Without belonging, you are crippled. In belonging, there is hope:

> "So now there is no condemnation for those who belong to Christ Jesus. And because you belong to him, the power of the life-giving Spirit has freed you from the power of sin that leads to death" (Romans 12:1-2).

No condemnation. The word "condemnation" is courtroom language.[145] It's the idea of sentencing one to a prison term. It's time to get out of jail. It's time to throw open your prison door. It's a prison cell confining you to a life of defeat, guilt, destruction, and unhappiness. Embrace faith this very moment.

Perhaps your first step is to put your faith and trust in Jesus Christ alone. His life-giving Spirit will free you from the power of your sin. Putting your full faith in Jesus Christ brings belonging. This is the promise of Scripture:

"Therefore, since we have been made right in God's sight by faith, we have peace with God because of what Jesus Christ our Lord has done for us. Because of our faith, Christ has brought us into this place of undeserved privilege where we now stand, and we confidently and joyfully look forward to sharing God's glory" (Romans 5:1-2).

If you've never put your faith in Christ Jesus, may I encourage you to do so now? A simple prayer of faith, depending on Jesus, is the beginning of change. Simply pray,

"Dear God, my need for You is great. My sin is greater. My desire is for You. This very moment, I put my total faith in Your Son Jesus Christ and Him alone. I begin a new life in You starting right now. Change me into the person of excellence You've created me to become. Thank You for Your love."

In Jesus Christ, all kinds of eternal processes begin now in your life. One new process is re-creation. "This means that anyone who belongs to Christ has become a new person. The old life is gone; a new life has begun!" (2 Corinthians 5:17).

If you've enjoyed a relationship with Christ for a period of time, that process still lives within you regardless of your failings. Christ still lives within you. The process of re-creation was halted because of your choices to be re-created in another image other than God's. Perhaps, it's time to redirect your life to God. Pray this simple prayer:

God, I'm where I'm at because of my own fault. Sorry. I've really messed up. Please forgive me, Father. Thank You for not giving up on me. Thank You for loving me. Thank You for second, third, fourth, and more chances. Take this tainted person before You. I commit my life to You. I give my body, mind, and spirit to You. Create in me a clean heart, God. Renew a right spirit within me. Let me experience the joy once again of knowing You. Help me, oh God, to reflect Your excellence through me to those around me. So be it—Amen.

Strengthen your boundaries. Put your BACKS into it. The tools are before you. Master them. Build and establish your boundaries. Strong accountability provides safety. Confession redeems the heart. Knowledge brings clear understanding. And, godly sorrow brings your soul and God together. Put that dragon back behind its own wall never to cross your boundary again.

ABOUT THE AUTHOR

Dr. D. J. Mingo spent over twenty years in Africa with his wife Kathy raising their three sons. Pastoring, counseling, and assisting South Africans with varieties of challenges provided a formative process to help people. Addictions of every variety plagued many. The same addictions found in assaulting Africans existed in the American church too.

Clearly set Boundaries of BACKS were develop over three decades of assisting many asking for his assistance.

Don is a professional Coach in Life, Group, Leadership, and Missionary Coaching with Professional Christian Coaching Institute.

He also holds several certifications and training in Critical Incident Stress Management, Chaplaincy, Trauma Care, Grief Care, Depression Recovery, Fire Fighting, and other disciplines. His greatest passion is helping God's people live life as God intended; abundantly.

Don and Kathy currently travel extensively helping Christian missionaries, pastors, and leaders in almost any capacity requested. When home, they live with their oldest son, his spouse, and their eight children in Wisconsin. Yes, that is correct; eight children!

Don, and his wife Kathy, currently offer coaching and care for pastors, missionaries, multi-cultural workers, and those serving in the church. Their motto is: "Helping leaders survive and thrive in ministry serving longer and stronger."

More information is available at

www.re-vitalize.org

twitter: @ReVitalizeCare

Facebook.com/Re-Vitalize

ENDNOTES

1   All Scripture, unless otherwise noted, is cited from the New Living Translation copyright © 1996. Tyndale House Publishers, Inc., Wheaton, Illinois 60189.

2   http://www.christianity.com/1270946/

3   Also lookup 1 Corinthians 9:27

4   "Icky" is an old term, used often in Minnesota, especially in rural areas. It means something that is sickening or undesirable.

5   Ibid.

6   Matthew 15:18

7   Proverbs 23:7

8   Proverbs 4:23

9   Hebrews 13:4

10   James 1:14-16

11   http://www.desiringgod.org/articles/sexual-sin-in-the-ministry

12 Steve Farrar, Finishing Strong (Colorado Springs, CO: Multnomah Publishers, 1995) page 72.

13   Ibid.

14   http://intimacyinmarriage.com/2014/02/20/5-reasons-the-church-wont-talk-authentically- about-sex/

15   James 5:16

16   http://www.crosswalk.com/church/pastors-or-leadership/how-many-porn-addicts-are-in- your-church-1336107.html

17   http://www.covenanteyes.com/2013/02/19/pornography-statistics/

18   http://18www.blazinggrace.org/open-letter-from-chuck-swindoll/

19   http://www.provenmen.org/

20   http://www.provenmen.org/2014pornsurvey/pornuseatwork/

21   http://www.provenmen.org/2014pornsurvey/christian-porn-stats/

22   Ibid.

23   Ibid.

24   Ibid.

25   http://www.desiringgod.org/articles/sexual-sin-in-the-ministry

26   http://www.crosswalk.com/church/pastors-or-leadership/how-many-porn-addicts-are-in- your-church-1336107.html

27   http://www.provenmen.org/2014pornsurvey/pornuseatwork/

28   http://iamatreasure.com/about-us/statistics/

29   http://www.internetsafety101.org/pornographystatistics.htm

30   http://www.covenanteyes.com/pornstats/

31   Ibid.

32   http://www.covenanteyes.com/2008/10/28/ex-porn-star-tells-the-truth-about-the-porn- industry/

33   https://www.lifesitenews.com/news/gq-magazine-tells-men-quit-watching-porn-before-it- ruins-your-sex-life

34   https://www.lifesitenews.com/blogs/porn-is-transforming-our-men-from-protectors-into- predators.-fight-back

35   http://www.covenanteyes.com/pornstats/

36   http://www.telegraph.co.uk/news/science/science-news/8499409/Internet-porn- encourages-sex-offenders.html

37   http://www.huffingtonpost.com/stephen-arterburn/sexually-incompetent-men-b_4086075.html

38   http://www.equip.org/article/the-effects-of-porn-on-the-male-brain-3/#christian-books-2

39   https://www.psychologytoday.com/blog/inside-porn-addiction/201111/can-pornography- trigger-depression

40   Can Pornography Trigger Depression? | Psychology Today https://www.psychologytoday.com/blog/inside-porn-addiction/201111/can-pornography-trigger-depression

41   http://www.mensjournal.com/health-fitness/health/are-you-watching-too-much-porn-20130821

42   Ibid

43   Ibid.

44   http://www.westernjournalism.com/shocking-new-study-finds-link-pornography-declining- marriage-rates/

45   http://www.mensjournal.com/health-fitness/health/are-you-watching-too-much-porn-20130821

46   Ibid.

47   Ibid.

48   http://fightthenewdrug.org/category/get-the-facts/brain/#sthash.eGPLKXpu.
     dpbs

49   Ibid.

50   http://www.fightthenewdrug.org/porn-changes-the-brain/#sthash.7ZzUJr0f.
     g9okpTmy.dpbs

51   http://www.megmeekermd.com/2015/02/a-psychiatrists-letter-to-young-
     people-about-fifty- shades-of-grey/

52   http://www.forbes.com/sites/crime/2012/06/23/is-fifty-shades-of-grey-
     dangerous/ Is 'Fifty Shades Of Grey' Dangerous? June 23, 2012.

53   https://www.addiction.com/expert-blogs/can-porn-addiction-cause-male-
     sexual- dysfunction/

54   http://www.christianity.com/1270946/

55   http://www.webmd.com/sexual-conditions/features/is-sex-addiction-real

56   http://www.studylight.org/desk/interlinear.cgi?ref=47005001

57   Ibid.

58   http://www.studylight.org/lexicons/greek/gwview.cgi?n=1398

59   Ibid.

60   http://www.usatoday.com/story/news/nation/2015/02/11/child-exploitation-
     dark-web- prisoner/22100993/

61   Ibid.

62   Ibid.

63   Ibid.

64   Helps Word-Studies copyright © 1987, 2011 by Helps Ministries, Inc.

65   COPYRIGHT ©2015 Grace to You - http://www.gty.org/resources/print/
     sermons/GTY112

66   Romans 6:20

67   John 15:15

68   Scott Carson, Mortal Combat (Burlington, Wisconsin: Sunday Morning
     Message Grace Church, April 19, 2015).

69   http://www.barnesandnoble.com/w/the-pirate-primer-george-
     choundas/1111430611 pg 92.

70   http://www.comrades.com/

71   "Donning" is a term for putting one's turnout gear or fire gear on properly.

72   http://www.preceptaustin.org/ephesians_614-15.htm

73   http://www.whatisneuroplasticity.com/pathways.php

74   How to Rewire Your Brain for Success. Published May 19, 2014 http://www.inc.com/geoffrey- james/use-neuroscience-to-make-you-successful.html

75   Michael   Specter   –   "Partial   Recall"   http://www.newyorker.com/magazine/2014/05/19/partial-recall New Yorker; May 19, 2014.

76   Psalm 46:1

77   Psalm 91:2

78   Psalm 61:3

79   Psalm 18:2

80   Psalm 144:2

81   Acts 17:28

82   2 Timothy 2:13

83   1 Corinthians 10:13

84   Proverbs 3:5-6

85   http://odb.org/2009/01/31/a-breach-in-the-wall/?shared=email&msg=fail

86   www.adblockplus.org

87   Psychological Science in the Public Interest - January 2012 vol. 13 no. 1 3-66

88   http://fightthenewdrug.org/photos-of-sex-trafficked-women-on-tinder-shows-this-crime-is- everywhere/#sthash.Fh0NFRky.TNcUqX0Z.dpbs

89   Celebrate Recovery is a wonderful program assisting many people struggling with various addictions. No criticism of that organization is intended here.

90   I Corinthians 10:13

91   Titus chapter 2

92   http://professionalchristiancoaching.com/

93   http://www.coachfederation.org/

94   http://professionalchristiancoaching.com/

95   http://christianlifecoaching.com/

96   http://www.celebraterecovery.com/

97   http://grouplocator.crgroups.info/

98   The other Repentance Psalms are: 6, 38, 102, 130, and 143.

99   1 Corinthians 10:11

100 2 Samuel 23

101 Journal of the Adventist Theological Society, 17/2 (Autumn 2006): 81–95. Article copyright

102 © 2006 by Richard M. Davidson.

103 http://www.jewishencyclopedia.com/articles/2659-bath-sheba

104 1 Samuel 11 & 12

105 Hebrews 12:6

106 Genesis 3

107 Genesis 4 107 Book of Jonah 108 Joshua 7

108 Proverbs 15:3

109 Proverbs 15:3

110 Matthew 25,23; Revelation 6:9-10; 2 Timothy 4:8; 1 Corinthians 9:25-27; James 1:12;

111 Revelation 2:10; 1 Peter 5:2-4; Philippians 3:12-14; Revelation 2, 3 & 21.

112 Psalm 51:16-17

113 Genesis 1:27

114 1 John 1:9 (MSG)

115 This article first appeared in *Christian Research Journal*, volume 34, number 05 (2011). For further information or to subscribe to the *Christian Research Journal* go to: http://www.equip.org

116 https://youtu.be/1Ya67aLaaCc

117 Ibid.

118 2 Corinthians 11:4

119 http://en.wikipedia.org/wiki/Leprosy

120 http://www.gq.com/blogs/the-feed/2013/11/10-reasons-why-you-should-quit-watching- porn.html

121 http://www.huffingtonpost.com/2013/12/11/naomi-wolf-porn_n_4428180.html Posted: 12/11/2013 6:26 pm EST Updated: 01/23/2014 1:38 am EST

122 Proverbs 6:23 (The Message)

123 Proverbs 14:2

124 http://fightthenewdrug.org/photos-of-sex-trafficked-women-on-tinder-shows-this-crime-is- everywhere/#sthash.Fh0NFRky.TNcUqX0Z.dpbs

125 Development Services Group, Inc., under Cooperative Agreement #2013– JF–FX–K002, http://www.ojjdp.gov/mpg/litreviews/CSECSexTrafficking.pdf

126 http://iamatreasure.com/about-us/statistics/#sthash.loteIWz4.dpbs

127 http://fightthenewdrug.org/photos-of-sex-trafficked-women-on-tinder-shows-this-crime-is- everywhere/#sthash.Fh0NFRky.lK4WgoPQ.dpbs

128 http://www.ojjdp.gov/mpg/litreviews/CSECSexTrafficking.pdf

129 Hughes, Donna M. 1999. Pimps and Predators on the Internet: Globalizing the Sexual Exploitation of Women and Children. New York, N.Y.: Coalition Against Trafficking in Women. http://www.uri.edu/artsci/wms/hughes/pprep.htm

130 Ibid. http://www.uri.edu/artsci/wms/hughes/ppcpt2.htm

131 Ibid.

132 http://www.bbc.com/news/technology-27885502

133 Ibid.

134 *The Message* (**MSG**) Copyright © 1993, 1994, 1995, 1996, 2000, 2001, 2002 by Eugene H. Peterson

135 James 1:16-17

136 Revelation 21:4

137 Romans 6:5-11

138 Again, there is no criticism of mental health professionals and Substance Abuse Counselors who use this clinical term.

139 Romans 8:1

140 http://www.studylight.org/desk/interlinear.cgi?ref=42015007

141 http://www.medicinenet.com/script/main/art.asp?articlekey=40362

142 https://en.wikipedia.org/wiki/Worship

143 http://www.enaretos.com/Enaretos/Enaretos.html

144 https://books.google.com/books?id=ltZBUW_F9ogC&pg=PA242&lpg=PA242&dq=epainos+in+the+new+testament&source=bl&ots=4BSBQTrMau&sig=fwDGeR8JjJRRKaCGHrcsMuwtWXs&hl=en&sa=X&ved=0CD4Q6AEwBmoVChMI1cXr-ZDMxwIVBaMeCh04jQtZ#v=onepage&q=epainos%20in%20the%20new%20testament&f=false

145 http://www.gotquestions.org/no-condemnation.html

NOTES

www.ingramcontent.com/pod-product-compliance
Lightning Source LLC
LaVergne TN
LVHW020928090426
835512LV00020B/3270